Rethinking Technology
in Schools
PRIMER

PETER LANG
New York • Washington, D.C./Baltimore • Bern
Frankfurt am Main • Berlin • Brussels • Vienna • Oxford

Vanessa Elaine Domine

Rethinking Technology in Schools PRIMER

PETER LANG
New York • Washington, D.C./Baltimore • Bern
Frankfurt am Main • Berlin • Brussels • Vienna • Oxford

Library of Congress Cataloging-in-Publication Data

Domine, Vanessa Elaine.
Rethinking technology in schools primer / Vanessa Elaine Domine.
p. cm. — (Peter Lang primers)
Includes bibliographical references and index.
1. Educational technology—United States—Evaluation.
2. Education—Effect of technological innovations on—United States.
3. Education—Aims and objectives—United States.
4. Technology and children--United States. I. Title.
LB1028.3.D646   371.33—dc22   2006101472
ISBN 978-0-8204-8800-4

Bibliographic information published by **Die Deutsche Bibliothek**.
Die Deutsche Bibliothek lists this publication in the "Deutsche
Nationalbibliografie"; detailed bibliographic data is available
on the Internet at http://dnb.ddb.de/.

Cover design by Clear Point Designs

© 2009 Peter Lang Publishing, Inc., New York
29 Broadway, 18th floor, New York, NY 10006
www.peterlang.com

Printed in the United States of America

Contents

Introduction

Imagine that you are a substitute teacher. You arrive at your seventh-grade classroom one morning and a colleague logs you onto the computer at the teacher's station in the front of the room. You then make a quick trip to the restroom before classes begin. When you return, you find two students using the computer and you promptly tell them to stop and take their seats for class to begin. As students enter the room you notice **pop-up windows** filled with pornographic images appearing on your computer screen. You click to close the windows, but each time you do, another window opens to display more pornographic images. Unsure of what to do, you admonish students to stay in their seats, but some curious students manage to get a glimpse of what is on the computer screen. It is lunchtime before you are able to leave the classroom to ask for help. Frantically, you ask teachers in the faculty lounge what to do. Nonchalantly, they tell you this sort of thing happens all the time and not to worry. You later notify the principal of what happened. Instead of finding a resolution or getting any assistance, you are arrested.

When your case eventually goes to trial, you discover that the computer in your classroom lacked effective security protection.

Pop-up windows occur when certain web sites open a new web browser window to interrupt the web page in view to display information usually in the form of an advertisement.

The district's license for the content filter had lapsed due to an incorrect email address. From the evidence presented, you also learn that the web site accessed by the students prior to class had a link that infected the computer with **malware**. Consequently, the internet browser on your machine was "porn trapped," which explains why clicking on the pop-up windows led to the display of more obscene images. Despite what you and many others see as negligence on the part of the technology coordinator, according to the Computer Decency Act (CDA), the district cannot be held liable for any harm caused by material that comes through the internet. Instead, you are convicted on four counts of risk of injury to a minor and face up to 40 years in prison. Needless to say, your professional and personal lives are turned upside down. You find it difficult to fathom this conviction. Afterall, your purpose for becoming a teacher was to help children, not to injure them.

> **Malware**
> is software intended to disable or damage a computer without the owner's knowledge.

This disturbing case actually occurred in 2004, when Julie Amero, a substitute teacher in Connecticut, found herself the helpless victim of technology gone awry during the school day. Although tragic, the case itself is fascinating particularly in the wake of the protest that ensued after her prosecution and conviction. On March 6, 2007, a $2,400 advertisement appeared in the *Hartford Courant* signed by 28 computer science professors who claimed Amero could not have controlled the pornographic pop-ups. It is significant that Amero's sentencing was delayed four times, which only suggests that the judge in this case was not satisfied with the original investigation. On June 6, 2007, the conviction was vacated and Amero was granted a new trial. Faced with a public relations nightmare, it is highly unlikely that the state attorney will pursue a new trial.

The case of Julie Amero raises questions for even the most tech-savvy of teachers: "What does it mean to be a technologically literate educator?" "What are our moral responsibilities as educators when it comes to navigating the unintended consequences of technology in the classroom?" The Amero case conveys a powerful message that internet access in school not only places students at risk, but also is pedagogically, professionally, and personally detrimental to teachers. Rather than assume risk, many teachers and administrators simply avoid it altogether by not using the internet in the classroom during the school day. However, relegating the uses

Internet filtering software is a software designed to control or restrict objectionable content delivered over the World Wide Web to a particular computer or network.

Acceptable Use Policy (AUP) is a set of rules applied by school districts that restrict the ways in which the internet may be used.

Technological literacy is broadly defined as the ability to understand and evaluate technology in order to function in society.

of the internet to nonschool contexts is equally problematic for teachers. Currently, teachers nationwide are facing harsh penalties and even job termination for posting inappropriate content and portrayals of their personal life on the very public social networking sites MySpace and Facebook. Although a common policy is to ban student access to social networking sites from school networks, it is not an educational solution. Prohibition may still be a wise option considering the lack of technological proficiency of many administrators and teachers coupled with the legal liability of school districts. In addition, mandatory **internet filtering software** and the establishment of **Acceptable Use Policies** (AUPs) may be prudent measures given the existence of online predators and cyberbullies. However, filters and policies do not entirely block inappropriate content from ultimately reaching the school classroom or the students—many of whom know how to bypass filters and gain access through proxy web sites. What is left unaddressed is the fact that filtering software is not entirely accurate. Content that is appropriate, even essential, to education is also unintentionally blocked in the process.

The prosecution of Julie Amero resonates with all teachers who have at some point in their careers felt powerless in the face of computers and the internet in the classroom. This pressure has steadily increased along with the standardization of technology in education. In 2000, the International Society for Technology in Education (ISTE) unveiled the National Educational Technology Standards for Students (NETS-S) and then later added standards for teachers (NETS-T) and also administrators (NETS-A). When Congress passed the No Child Left Behind Act in 2002, it mandated that all students in the United States achieve **technological literacy** by the end of eighth grade, with states administering their own standardized tests beginning in 2007. Fostering technological literacy is an uphill battle, given the lack of professional development among teachers, the simultaneous push for Highly Qualified teachers (in subject areas rather than technology pedagogy), and the administrative focus on policy restrictions rather than instructional practices. The 2008 *Technology Counts* report reveals that, in the United States, 95 percent of fourth grade students and 83 percent of eighth grade students have access to computers. However, only five states test students on technology and only

19 states include technology in their initial teacher licensure requirements. The mean score across all 50 states (in terms of technology access, use, and capacity in schools) is merely average (76.9 percent). In a highly industrialized country where the technology industry dominates, it is paradoxical that U.S. schools are technologically anemic.

Few will disagree that the primary purpose of technology in schools should be educational empowerment rather than instructional oppression. However, the lack of technology professional development, coupled with the increased risk of students accessing harmful content during the school day, poses significant challenges for schooling. This book invites educators and all those who work in schools to linger in the paradox of technology in schools: The machines and tools that we celebrate, embrace, and implement in our lives inside and outside the classroom are also the vehicles for the very things we abhor: terrorism, commercialism, cyberbullying, plagiarism, and child pornography, just to name a few. The story of Julie Amero is a cautionary tale for all educators: We can no longer consider technology to be nothing more than value-free tools to deliver curriculum. To do so is to equate learning with mere information acquisition without understanding how to evaluate, produce, communicate, or contextualize such information. The chapters that follow redefine technology in schools and offer teachers, administrators, leaders, and policymakers models for technology leadership as well as for curriculum and technology integration.

Throughout the book, I intentionally address teachers as the primary audience, as they are at the forefront of education on a daily basis. Like Julie Amero, they have the most at stake personally, professionally, and pedagogically. However, I address these ideas to administrators, principals, technology coordinators, and library media specialists as well. Together, these educators can rethink school as a place where content and form of technology are not only technically mastered but also fundamentally questioned. As the case of Julie Amero suggests, the freedoms and dangers associated with the internet present moral and legal quandaries that require more complex solutions than merely equipping computers with internet filters and/or young people with technical skills. We need what Neil Postman describes as an overarching narrative—a story that constructs necessary ideals,

rules of conduct, sources of authority, and purpose that are absent in the digital universe yet absolutely essential to education. The following pages are a prologue to a new narrative for technology in schools.

Glossary

Pop-up windows—occur when certain web sites open a new web browser window to interrupt the web page in view to display information usually in the form of an advertisement.

Malware—is software intended to disable or damage a computer without the owner's knowledge.

Internet filtering software—is a software designed to control or restrict objectionable content delivered over the World Wide Web to a particular computer or network.

Acceptable Use Policy (AUP)—is a set of rules applied by school districts that restrict the ways in which the internet may be used.

Technological literacy—is broadly defined as the ability to understand and evaluate technology in order to function in society.

CHAPTER ONE

Technology Redefined

Technology
is a way of thinking
about information,
knowledge, and the
world at large.

Semantics
is the study of meaning
in communication.

The word **technology** was not always synonymous with computers. It was only after the Great Exhibition of 1851 in London that the word became exclusively associated with machines. The word *technology* in its original context denotes know-how or method, not necessarily for the purpose of advancing knowledge but mainly for the purpose of solving technical problems. These **semantics** are key to unlocking the current cultural meaning of the term. In other words, educators can neither talk about nor act intelligently with technology without first identifying assumptions, expectations, and goals for schooling. Rethinking technology in schools requires that we first agree on the definition of key terms.

Misunderstanding the word *technology* is closely linked to the misuses and even non-uses of it in schools. Most educators hear the word *technology* and conjure up images of sophisticated, mysterious, expensive digital devices (such as computers, the internet, digital cameras, electronic whiteboards, and mp3 players). Indeed, the word itself is enshrouded with such mystery that it frequently commands respect and even awe. Many teachers ruefully confess, "I don't really use any technology in my teaching."

Yet such a statement reveals a lack of understanding the fundamental principle that all curriculum is mediated by some form of technology—whether pen, book (printing press), film, or internet. In the classroom context, the curriculum cannot be separated from the technology through which it is constituted.

Technology as Language

Arguably the most important tool for human existence is language. It is essential for human thought and understanding. All of life's activities are conducted through some form of language. Language is the vehicle through which knowledge is shaped, transformed, and communicated to others. Without language, we have no means of understanding the world, since our way of thinking is inextricably linked to our way of speaking. It is through our everyday uses of language that we negotiate our individual and collective identities and navigate the world around us. In this sense, language is more than just a vehicle for transmitting messages—it both conveys and constitutes a particular stance towards the world. In this way, language can never be neutral since it imposes both a point of view about the world and also a way of seeing the world. At the same time, our speech is never entirely our own. We are constantly incorporating the words of others into our own discourse. In this sense, just as humans use language, language uses us. It is, therefore, requisite that educators look more closely at the language that consistutes curriculum and the curriculum constructed through language.

The construction of knowledge is both a social process and a symbolic process. Technology is a powerful mediator of communication as it provides humans with symbols and systems that assist in the construction of knowledge. Technology can, therefore, be defined as methodology or a process of doing things that lends itself to a particular way of seeing and thinking about the world. It cannot refer to value-free tools that can be picked up and put down at will. In a much larger sense, technology is a way of thinking about information, knowledge, and the world at large.

Similarly, technology is a way of thinking about curriculum. As such, its uses in education can never be neutral because it presents not only a particular view of the world, but also how

people learn about the world. Textbooks, newspapers, maps, magazines, film, TV, videos, computers, internet, and cameras are just a few of the ways teachers and students shape and reflect curriculum. All supply students and teachers with powerful symbolic materials from which to negotiate meaning. It is, therefore, inaccurate to think of computers, films, TV, and even the chalkboard as merely tools for transmitting curriculum since information cannot be separated from the medium through which it is communicated.

Technology as Media

Epistemologies
are theories of knowledge that address what constitutes knowledge, how it is acquired, and what people know.

Media scholars have already established that oral, print, electronic, and digital communication media carry with them different **epistemologies** that in turn structure our individual and collective ways of knowing. This can be illustrated through an analysis of television as both a technology and a medium for communication. Technically speaking, television is an electronic box with a window on the front. For many, the TV is also a furniture accessory around which all other home decor is configured. Its useability includes a variety of functions that place control in the hand of the viewer. The viewer can interrupt programming using a remote control (e.g., to skip advertisements or to record a program for playback later). The viewer can also alter picture and sound quality and activate the **v-chip** in order to filter programming content. With the emergence of digital video recorders, viewing TV is no longer a linear activity where a viewer must watch a program from beginning to end. Viewers can skip to any part in the program at any time. With the continuous development of technologies, viewers can increase their ability to control and interact with programming. However, consumer power is counteracted through the inherent obsolescence of technology. In the case of TV, obsolescence will be particularly troublesome for those who will not convert from analog TV receivers to digital TV receivers by 2009 when the analog signal transmission will cease.

V-chip
is a viewer control technology incorporated into television receivers that allows parents to manage or block their children's television viewing. It operates on a programming code that indicates the violence, sex, and language rating of programming.

Medium
is any channel or tool through which communication occurs.

The conversation deepens when we talk about television as a **medium** for mass communication. At school, work, and in social settings we report to others what we watched or who we voted for (or against) in the latest reality program. We share perspectives on specific episodes, characters, events, and even

commercial advertisements. Many viewers are unaware that television technology was originally created for the purpose of commercial advertising. Television allows marketers to communicate to consumers on a mass scale through the sponsorship of programming content. An extreme example is the broadcast of the Superbowl football game, which in 2009 will command $US 3 million per 30 seconds of advertising. Television is inherently a market-driven, for-profit medium for communicating between advertisers and a mass audience of consumers. From this perspective, television programming addresses all audience members as consumers. Therefore, promoting the values of **consumerism** and competition is essential for television producers in ensuring an audience for programming content. Many viewers are not aware of this potentially oppressive scenario of television institutions reigning over target audiences. The idea is to be fully aware of the biases and constraints of television, so as to not expect the medium of television to be something that it cannot be technologically. It is, therefore, illogical (although not out of the question) to expect broadcast TV programming within schools to be anything other than commercially biased. More about the influences of commercial media in schools is discussed in Chapter 2.

The educational power and potential of recent technological advancements lie in their multimedia, nonlinear, and interactive capabilities. Access to **multimedia** already existed through television to the extent that programming content relied on the interaction of text, audio, and video (multimedia forms) to create meaning. TV programming is also interactive media in the sense that the multimedia forms interact to create meaning. However, from a technical perspective, one can argue there is very little tangible interaction between viewer and traditional **analog** TV programming. That is, although the audience may actively observe and make meaning of programming content, they traditionally had little control or choice in the viewing experience. As technology evolved, the remote control provided much more control and choice in the hand of the viewer. **Audience interactivity** (as distinct from media interactivity) dramatically increased when the technology empowered the viewer to navigate digital video recording, skip advertisements, and locate individual chapters within a DVD, for example.

Consumerism
equates the pursuit of happiness with the purchase of material possessions.

Multimedia
is the use of more than one medium of expression or communication.

Analog
refers to communication signals that are used in their original form. In contrast, digital communication turns analog signals into numbers that are stored on a digital device.

Audience interactivity
is the active user participation afforded by multimedia. Such interactivity implies the occurance of two-way communication.

Closed captioning
allows hearing-impaired people to access program content through text captions or subtitles that are displayed and that transcribe speech and other sounds.

Telenovela
is a popular type of Spanish soap opera.

WebTV
was a consumer technology developed in the mid-1990s that used television for display of World Wide Web content rather than a computer monitor.

World Wide Web
is a system of interlinked hypertext documents that are accessed via the internet.

We can take the analysis even further by looking at how the technological features of television influence its media (or communication) characteristics. **Closed captioning** is just one technological feature of television. Yet its implications for television as a communication medium are significant. Combining text with video provides hearing-impaired audiences access to programming. Subtitles blend text, video, and audio in a way that provides all audiences with an added layer of literal meaning and access to language and grammar. In another context, an English-speaking viewer might learn Spanish by regularly watching closed-captioned episodes of a **telenovela**, where the situational drama (video) and vocal intonation (audio) combine to form contextual clues to facilitate the viewer's understanding of the textual narrative. Along similar lines, the popular and longstanding public television program *Sesame Street* maximizes the multimedia features of television technology to cultivate literacy among young children. By combining text with video and audio (usually through song), the viewer has multiple modes of access to written and spoken language. Just as we recognize structural qualities of a written essay, it is important to acknowledge the structural qualities of a multimedia text.

The possibilities of media are also accompanied by constraints. In the case of television, it is primarily two-dimensional and linear. With the exception of **WebTV**, the screen is flat (and these days, flatter is better) and most audiences cannot interact with the program as they can with content on the **World Wide Web,** or relive a news broadcast. Most audiences can achieve only a moderate amount of interactivity with TV, as they record programming on-demand. Highly interactive programming requires additional technologies that allow audiences to vote and decide the outcome of a particular program. This type of audience voting is usually accomplished through telephone or text messaging and not through the TV itself. We must also be wary of the illusory nature of television and other screen technologies. The integration of images, sounds, and texts creates a media-rich illusion of reality that constructs a sense of intimacy and connection to one another—as if we are actually there and are experiencing reality first-hand. In reality, we are disconnected and distanced from reality and in some cases even duped.

This multimedia and interactive design is both enhanced and enabled through the nonlinear features of digital media, specifically the World Wide Web. In contrast to a linear slide show or a live television broadcast, **hypermedia** allows users to essentially design their own experience— choosing where to begin, the sequence of events, and what to experience. On the web, this is known as "surfing." Originally, the World Wide Web was hypertext, which allowed the connection of textual information based on conceptual linkages rather than a linear or chronological format. Hypermedia combines multimedia forms (image, video, audio, text) and allows the user much choice (and serendipitous opportunity) in accessing and experiencing information, given there is no longer a prescribed "storybook" beginning or ending. The educational implications for accessing information are tremendous; even more impressive are the opportunities for the user to organize, manipulate, produce, and utilize information in ways never before possible. A single user can manipulate digital information (i.e., document, image, audio, or video file) to create a new original and at the same time leave the original artifact intact. It is, therefore, essential that humans understand not only how to access information but also how to organize it, evaluate it, and produce it in ways that are lawful, ethical, and socially responsible.

Given that our daily conversations about television and other technologies most likely exist at the level of content (i.e., programs, episodes, web sites), we are less likely as individual users to achieve **transparency** when it comes to how the biases of technology influence human communication. The absence of nonverbal signals (i.e., vocal intonation, inflection, and facial expressions) in email exchanges frequently lead to miscommunication and even heated arguments based on textual information alone. This gap in communication places serious constraints on the uses of email to navigate human relationships. However, making such technical constraints transparent allows the user to intelligently select the most accurate medium and technology for communicative purposes. Communicative competence is a double-edged sword, however. There are users who intentionally end social relationships through email precisely to avoid such nonverbal intimacy and social accountability.

Hypermedia

is an extension of hypertext where graphics, audio, video, text, and hyperlinks work together to create a nonlinear medium for communication.

Transparency

refers to the explicit understanding on the part of the user as to the ways in which technological characteristics impact communication.

PowerPoint
is a computer software program widely used in business and education as a tool for making presentations.

Unfortunately, both ignorance of and fixation on the constraints of technology can sabotage our communications goal. Take, for example, the common criticisms of **PowerPoint** presentation software. Technologically, PowerPoint is a useful visual aid that allows a speaker to abbreviate ideas. It can provide a colorful presentation, leading an audience through a complex series of concepts. At the same time, PowerPoint tends to shut down conversation, rather than facilitate it. The responsibility for stimulating discussion, therefore, lies with the presenter or orator. The technical features of PowerPoint are also significant. The creation of slides requires decision making about what multimedia information (text, image, sound, movie, transitions) to place on each slide. This requires the orator or producer to possess a knowledge base of the audience, presentation timeframe, and a clear vision of what ideas to express. The possibilities and constraints of PowerPoint software remind us that educational innovation lies not in the technology itself, but in the educator's understanding of curriculum and how the instructional technology shapes both the curricular message and the student's understanding of the message.

Technology as Bureaucracy

The goals of educational technology over the past 25 years include ensuring the future employment of today's youth and maintaining the economic and political dominance of the United States. The focus on twenty-first century job skills is, to a certain extent, understandable as it is of continual concern to educators and employers in the United States. The U.S. Bureau of Labor Statistics projects that by 2014 the growth of jobs in the area of computer systems design and information will exceed 40 percent (more than three times faster than the average for all occupations). The Bureau also projects that employment of computer and mathematical science workers across industries will grow faster than the average for all occupations and that three out of ten new jobs will be in computer systems design and related services. Such an economic imperative is a powerful incentive for educators and policymakers to produce high school graduates highly skilled in the areas of math, science, and technology.

Unfortunately, the goal of all students achieving technological literacy by the end of eighth grade is fixated on a moving

E-rate

is part of the federal Universal Service Fund authorized as part of the Telecommunications Act of 1996. It provides discounts to assist schools and libraries in the United States to obtain affordable telecommunications and internet access. E-rate is funded through a Universal Service fee charged to companies that provide telecommunications services.

Digital divide

is the gap between those people with access to information technology equipment (usually via computers and the internet) and the associated skills and those without access to it.

No Child Left Behind (NCLB)

is a U.S. federal law passed in 2001 that reauthorized a number of federal programs aimed at improving the performance of K-12 schooling through increasing the standards of accountability for states, school districts, and schools.

target that may not be attainable for all. The mere obsolescence of technology creates huge financial stumbling blocks for schools. Paradoxically, the federal government promotes "data-driven decision-making" to improve student learning through the use of technology systems, yet at the same time schools lack access to those electronic data and analytical knowledge needed to inform and actually transform classroom practice.

For families and individuals who reside on the lower rungs of the socioeconomic ladder, technology is tangential and perhaps even inconsequential to their survival. In an attempt to increase equitable access to the internet, the U.S. government in 1997 subsidized a $2 billion program called **E-rate** (Educational Rate) to help schools and libraries obtain internet wiring and services. E-rate provided up to a 90 percent discount to schools with the largest number of poor children. The goal of E-rate was to increase equity of access, that is, to bridge the **digital divide** across poor and wealthy communities within the United States; however, the attempt was not without controversy and suspicion of widespread fraud and abuse within the administration of the program. Reportedly 99 percent of schools (not classrooms) in the United States now have access to the internet. While nearly all schools have some level of internet access, the digital divide remains a reality in the homes of many students within urban communities. As of 2005, only 25 percent of the poorest households in the United States had internet access, compared with 80 percent of homes with annual incomes above $75,000. The paradox of E-rate is that although poorer school districts now have increased access to technology, they also have increased chances of failure without equal access to professional development and technical support—both beyond the scope of E-rate.

These bureaucratic goals echo in the present through the discourse of increased accountability imbued by the 2002 **No Child Left Behind** (NCLB) Act. The U.S. Department of Education (through NCLB) funds the costs of standardized testing while simultaneously cutting funds to preexisting Technology Innovation Challenge Grants and the Technology Literacy Challenge—both national funding streams that in the past supported thoughtful and integrative uses of technology in schools and communities. Instead, the Enhancing Education through Technology (EETT) portion of NCLB defines

technological literacy as the ability to use computers to communicate, locate and manage information, and to use these tools effectively to support learning. Its primary purpose is skills acquisition in order to increase achievement in other academic subjects—particularly in math and science. However, this skills-based approach is imbalanced in favor of an economic rather than educational imperative. Technology is narrowly defined as computers, excluding the powerful learning that can and does occur through oral, print, video, and other analog media forms. *Literacy* is also narrowly defined in this case, as it does not include the recognition and understanding of one's own purposes for thinking and communicating and for selecting technology accordingly.

To facilitate technological literacy under No Child Left Behind the U.S. government in 2004 unveiled a National Educational Technology Plan (NETP) that promotes, in part, ubiquitous access to computers and **connectivity** for each student. The NETP promotes high-speed connectivity and distance learning for the purpose of increasing math and science achievement and for securing our nation's future. The NETP is a self-proclaimed, technology-driven educational reform, in contrast to educationally driven renewal with the assistance of technology. The balance is further weighted towards industry and economics through the NETP's rationale that young people will be able to exploit new technologies to enter the workforce and be economically competitive.

The technological literacy challenge is further complicated by the curricular confusion between technology education and educational technology—two separate fields of study that embody different purposes for and approaches to schooling. Technology education focuses more on the manipulation of materials and tools to shape the physical world. Technology education standards are based on a separate set of technological literacy standards developed by the National Science Foundation (NSF) and the National Aeronautics and Space Administration (NASA). It is, therefore, in the best (economic) interests of the computer, science, and aeronautics industries for schools to produce graduates who are technologically literate and, therefore, mandate it as a separate curriculum subject area. In contrast, the field of educational technology is concerned with the integration of concepts, skills, operations, and ethics pertaining to technology across all

Connectivity

is the state of being connected or interconnected. It can refer to social and/or computing situations.

subject areas and grade levels. The goal is for students, teachers, and administrators to use technologies to support student learning. The pedagogical focus is not so much on learning *about* technology as it is on learning *with* technology.

No doubt the drive for accountability in the area of technological literacy is a boon for the technology industry, the corporate sector in general, and the educational testing industry. At the same time, there is little evidence that directly links technologies with improved teaching, learning, or even higher test scores. In fact, a recent congressionally mandated scientific study of the effectiveness of educational technology by the National Center for Education Evaluation concluded that the use of math and reading software produces no significant gains in test scores or student achievement. This is not surprising given the numerous policy reports over the past two decades that continuously call for higher quality content and software for education and the raising of offline and online content and applications to federal, state, and local standards. Ultimately, federal policies concerning technology in education ignore the fundamental principle that increased access to and accountability for student achievement and basic technological proficiency require systemic support and cannot be accurately assessed in terms of standardized tests scores or internet access.

The systematization of technology use through curriculum standardization may be one viable means to satisfy the needs of education (by raising academic standards) and industry (by rationalizing expenditures on equipment). One organizational body that blends the two worlds is the International Society for Technology in Education (ISTE), a collaborative of teachers, teacher educators, curriculum and education associations, government, businesses, and private foundations. The ISTE in 2000 established the National Educational Technology Standards for Students (NETS-S) and subsequently added sets of standards for teachers (NETS-T) and administrators (NETS-A). The NETS consist of performance indicators in the areas of operational proficiency; productivity; communication; research; problem solving; and social, ethical, and human issues. The NETS are innovative in several ways. In contrast to state standards (where such exists) that designate technological literacy as a separate subject area, the NETS position technology as integral to core subject area curricula and, therefore, an educational responsibility of students, teachers, and

administrators. Secondly, the NETS acknowledge the student as an active learner, privilege shared decision making, and recommend changes in the structure of school schedules (NETS-S, 2002). Among the NETS goals for students are preparing them for their future role as productive citizens, exciting students and teachers about their participation in that system, and organizing a continual process of change and flexibility. The emphasis on social, political, and technological change is mirrored in the recent move by ISTE to consult with educators across the United States and 22 other countries to revise the NETS for students and teachers. The revisions (see Appendices A and B) place additional emphasis on assessment of technology use and school improvement.

Federal bureaucrats are slow to acknowledge that technology-driven policies and skills-based standards are not enough for public education in the United States. In a 2006 press conference, Federal Communications Commissioner Michael Copps identified the need for a more critical and media-oriented approach to technology in schools:

> The more I grasp the pervasive influence of media on our children, the more I worry about the media literacy gap in our nation's educational curriculum. We need a sustained K-12 media literacy program—something to teach kids not only how to use the media but how the media uses them. Kids need to know how particular messages get crafted and why, what devices are used to hold their attention and what ideas are left out. In a culture where media is pervasive and invasive, kids need to think critically about what they see, hear and read. No child's education can be complete without this.

Commissioner Copps does not diminish the need for technological literacy (to do so would contradict the capitalistic culture into which students are preparing to enter). Instead, he calls for increased critical thinking among students and reframes technology as media for youth empowerment. Thus young people remain consumers of technology, with the addition of being more critical consumers. Copps statement does not take issue with whether or not young people would consume various types of media and technology. Rather, his concern is to produce the most educated consumers of media and technology—and to do so through the structures of K-12 schooling in the United States.

It is significant that the ideals of technology-driven educational reform cannot yet be fully realized when it comes to student achievement and standardized testing. Even those students who are predisposed to gaining or who eventually achieve high levels of technical proficiency do not necessarily possess the critical habits of mind to transform information into knowledge and then leverage that knowledge for public good. In short, students who are technologically literate (according to national and state standards) may possess technical ability but will not necessarily be compelled to think or act with technologies in ways that are socially, politically, or culturally responsible.

Media Literacy and Technology

Media literacy

is the ability to access, analyze, evaluate, produce, and communicate using a variety of media forms.

To truly empower students requires more than the current skills-based definition of technological literacy to include **media literacy**—the ability to access, analyze, evaluate, produce, and communicate through a variety of media and technology forms. Media literacy does not diminish the importance of technological proficiency; in fact, it necessitates it. However, it requires students, teachers, and administrators to go beyond a technical skill set toward a disposition of participatory citizenship.

There are many social activists who align themselves with media literacy and yet do not seek technological proficiency and may even reject and/or protest the proliferation of newer technologies. Ultimately, however, media literacy should *not* be spun as educational ludditism, as it is not about making value judgments on what technology is inherently "better" for teaching and learning. Instead, media literacy is about acknowledging the different codes and conventions relative to all forms of communications technology and the ways in which those media forms work together to construct messages. In the context of school, a media-literate teacher makes conscientious decisions about the uses of instructional technologies. When (s)he verbally explains the concept of metamorphosis using a pictorial illustration of a caterpillar, chrysalis, and butterfly, (s)he is aware that it is a different mediated experience as compared to accessing **streaming video** from the internet to illustrate the process of metamorphosis occurring. In this case, moving images provide a more realistic and detailed view for students as compared to still images. Granted, seeing the process live, firsthand, would be the most accurate and

Streaming video

refers to the delivery method of multimedia content over telecommunications networks. Video content is constantly displayed to the user while it is being delivered by the provider.

authentic of all learning experiences, but difficult to broadcast to all 30 students, who would most likely not get an up-close view. Whatever the curriculum or method of instruction, teachers and students can better understand the constructed nature of information (and, therefore, better understand their curriculum) if they get a clear understanding of the languages associated with instructional (and more broadly, educational) technology by analyzing and utilizing the languages of media.

How do teachers cultivate media literacy among their students? Media literacy is not something to be "added-on" as another subject area to teach. Rather, it is an interdisciplinary framework with which to contextualize all types of information. It operationalizes and contextualizes the nebulous phrases that appear in district and school mission statements: "develop critical thinkers," "cultivate responsible citizens," and the even more pervasive, "promote lifelong learning." In enacting this global vision of education, *all* teachers (not just the English teacher, computer teacher, or Art teacher) can and should integrate media literacy into their teaching. Although there exist different approaches to media literacy education, it can generally be represented through four governing principles corresponding to knowledge construction, media languages, ownership, and the interpretations of the audience or user.

Media technologies construct curriculum. Whether we employ books, radio, videos, pen to paper, computers, or the internet—each of these communication forms embodies a way of thinking that orients teachers and students to information (and the world at large) in a particular way. For example, the presence of a TV in the classroom suggests that knowledge and reality exist outside the classroom and are deliverable through a box plugged into the wall. The technology of TV privileges access to information over creation of knowledge. However, technology is ultimately con-textualized by the ways in which teachers choose to use it (or not to use it) within the classroom setting.

To separate curriculum content from technology form is not only false but endangers the very disciplines we purport to teach, as facades of normalcy are filtered through books, film, TV, and other instructional technology sources. Instructional technologies mediate curriculum and, therefore, construct reality for our students. From a media literacy perspective, TV is not a window to the

world, but rather a popular means of constructing culture and classroom curriculum. The media products of TV portray a particular view of actual people, places, events, and ideas. As part of their conventional form (or language), newspapers, magazines, television, and the internet use shortcuts to meaning, also known as stereotyping. Although a technical necessity, the consequences of stereotyping can be oppressive for groups (not) represented. Criticism is silenced through representations that most people assume to be normal and inevitable. Questions that elicit critical thinking about the texts of technology are, "Whose story is being told?" and "Whose story is being left out?"

Media literacy involves determining the degree to which the texts of technologies represent real life by determining how the people, places, events, and ideas represent a particular ideological view. For example, a two-minute news segment about the Americanization of Japan includes sound bytes from several Japanese citizens, in fluent English, praising Disneyland. This portrayal represents a particular set of assumptions about Japanese culture, American culture, the relationship between the two cultures, and what is considered news. From a critical perspective, the goal of identifying media (mis)representations is ultimately emancipatory: To set free those who are oppressed and change the social (and media) institutions that interfere with the democratic ideal.

Forms of language govern media technologies. Without language, we have no means of understanding the world, as it is our tool for developing human thought and understanding. The first step towards a **critical pedagogy** of technology is to understand that our curriculum cannot be separated from the technologies through which we teach. As teachers, we need to be aware that our choices of instructional technology reveal not only what we think students should learn, but also how we think students should learn. Jerome Bruner (1986) writes:

Critical pedagogy is an approach to teaching that helps students question and challenge the dominant social and political ideologies that are ultimately oppressive.

> The medium of exchange in which education is conducted—language—can never be neutral, that it imposes a point of view not only about the world to which it refers but toward the use of mind in respect of this world. Language necessarily imposes a perspective in which things are viewed and a stance toward what we view. It is not just, in the shopworn phrase, that the medium is the message. The message itself may create the reality that the message embodies and predispose those who hear it to think about it in a particular mode.

Media languages refer to the formal, technical, and aesthetic features of how a particular communications technology (through the manipulation of the user) produces and distributes meaning. Each communications technology has its own set of rules and unique ways in which it assists in the construction of meaning. Film producers construct meaning through editing, narration, sequencing, camera angles, soundtrack timing, and the combination of text, images, and sound. Magazine editors use different codes and conventions as compared to video producers as compared to web designers. Similarly, a commercial advertisement for Pringles potato chips during a Channel One news program uses different codes and conventions (e.g., fast-paced camera cuts, pop music dub, zoom-ins and zoom-outs) as compared to a Microsoft banner advertisement on a web site (e.g., flashing bold text alongside a question mark next to a Microsoft logo). It is through the analysis and production of media language(s) that students can better understand the constructed nature of information and the mediation of experiencing that information. Such awareness is essential, given the multisensory modalities of multimedia and hypermedia.

The ownership of media technologies influences curriculum content. Institutions own media technologies and have historical-social contexts usually (but not always) concealed from the general public. A magazine is a product of an institution consisting (in part) of a news corporation, the storywriters, photographers, a team of editors, and advertising and circulation departments. Similarly, a television program is constructed by a production company, scheduled by a programmer and broadcast by a network. Each of these institutional elements influences the content as well as audience interpretation of the content. The reality within the United States is the inherent nature of media and technology as corporate or institutionally (not individually) owned. Books, films, televisions, and computers are products of industry—owned and operated according to principles that will generate the highest profit, which usually involves addressing the largest audience. The **commodification** of technologies produces media content and curriculum that cater to a broader audience (to generate higher sales), rather than reflecting diversity of opinion. Media literacy poses the questions, "Who owns, produces, and distributes this technology? This information?" and ultimately, "Whose interests are served?"

Commodification
refers to the transformation of ideas and educational practices into commodities.

The educational testing industry situates students, schools, and even nations in competition with one another. The historical trend of curriculum standardization and acquisition of technology shapes and in turn is shaped by the market demands of the educational testing industry. If math and reading test scores plummet, educational administrators engage in hot pursuit of the latest computer-based technologies and/or pre-packaged curricula in a desperate attempt to raise test scores. Research reveals, however, no correlation between such technologies and student achievement in these areas.

Students interpret the texts and technologies of instruction. Surprisingly, most educational technology battles are not fought over whether to order more books or computers. Rather, they are fought within the arena of epistemology or how knowledge comes into being. Of paramount importance is a teacher's philosophical and pedagogical orientation to technologies as instructional media: that is, how educators view the communication (teaching-learning) process between information technology and its users or audiences. In the United States alone, there exist many different perspectives on how to educate youth with and about technology, but not all of them agree to what extent young people are active participants in the process. More often than not, teacher access to technology is limited to a traditional instructional model of information access and delivery. Often the source of knowledge is some type of equipment plugged into the wall or the lecture method or "drill-and-kill." This "plug-in" model of instruction reflects an epistemology of knowledge that can be plugged into the student's brain through a linear transfer of information.

Rather than knowledge as transmission of information, the interpretive paradigm defines knowledge as transformation that occurs in both social and symbolic ways. From this perspective, the construction of knowledge (teaching and learning) depends upon cultural context, student dialogue, and interaction with media texts and technologies. With curriculum, meaning does not reside in the "text" itself; rather meaning is a product of the interaction between the text and the audience. Audiences interpret meaning based on situational elements such as geography, culture, age, class, gender, time of day, and the context in which they interact with the text. Additionally, various media forms resonate in different ways, depending upon the experiences, values, and knowledge that audiences bring to it. For example, an impoverished minority urban adolescent in a crowded school classroom will not interpret a media text or situation in the same way as a middle class suburban youth who is one of fifteen students in a classroom. Although students differ in their perceptions, understandings, and reactions to media, the key is to educate them to be aware of the conditions surrounding their own subjectivity as well as the subjectivity of others.

The four principles of media literacy account for how knowledge is constructed, the nature of the relationship between audience/user and media/technology, and more specifically the ways in which curricula are impacted through various technology forms. The principles comprise a gateway into a deeper critical awareness of information and content, while also reflecting upon the impact of technology upon curriculum and student learning. As such, these four principles can be reconfigured as questions for teachers to pose directly to students, or as principles to govern curriculum development, including (but not limited to) technological literacy.

If technology is ideology, then educators must first identify whose interests are at stake, particularly during an age when more knowledge is available outside the four walls of the school classroom than inside. The possibility for political convergence of technological and media literacies is an open invitation for educators to decide which technologies are appropriate and which technologies empower and serve the felt needs of the local community. Horace Mann referred to this type of critical thinking as habits of mind that question, "How do we know what we know?" "Who is speaking?" "What causes what?" "How might things have been different?" and "Who cares?" The public school is one of the few places where the majority of young people can safely ask such questions. Yet a real tension exists between the bureaucratic realities of capitalism (and the economic motive driving technological literacy) in the United States and the social activist approach of media literacy that essentially resists capitalistic forces and the bureaucratic structures and processes of schooling. Given this tension, the definition of technological literacy must be expanded to include increased social and political aptitude among young people. Democratically speaking, just as the uses of technology should privilege diversity among students and within communities,

they should also privilege diversity of technologies (analog and digital alike) and teaching styles.

Technology as Democratic Practice

One of the purposes of education in the United States, at least according to Thomas Jefferson, was to provide all citizens with the knowledge and training that would enable us to pursue happiness and self-government. John Dewey also asserted nearly a century ago that schools should be sites where students can learn and practice social and civic participation. Known as **progressivism**, this philosophy of education assumes that students thrive intellectually and socially when they are active participants in their own learning. Progressivism logically requires that students move beyond the four walls of the classroom to interface with colleagues, families, and community agencies through service. Public education should, therefore, mentor students in the way of civic responsibility. However, the challenges of translating civic education into practices of **civic engagement** are chronic and are met with opposition. The American Democracy Project reports that in a society that is increasingly technologically connected, Americans actually feel disconnected from government and increasingly disconnected from one another. This challenge is exacerbated by increased immigration and an increased need to create a sense of collective commitment.

Just as technology can be thought of as a way of seeing the world, so can **democracy** be thought of as a process or way of thinking. From this perspective, democracy is much more than a curriculum destination. It is a set of values that guide individual lives. An ideal educational use of technology is to facilitate social, political, and economic connections among individuals, schools, and the larger world. Unfortunately, many classroom uses of technology (i.e., books, videos, internet, interactive whiteboards, PowerPoint, computer-based testing) reflect the dominant model of schooling as **cultural transmission** that decontextualizes information from its broader social, political, and economic meaning. Given the global nature of knowledge (both in terms of geography and scope of information) and the communal demands of democracy, it is essential for educators to foster critical habits of mind that enable students to access information from a variety of sources, evaluate that information, and analyze it to make decisions

Progressivism
is an educational philosophy that emphasizes democracy, student needs, practical activities, and school-community relationships.

Civic engagement
refers to individual and collective actions that identify and address issues of public concern.

Democracy
is a process that embodies the ideals of inquiry, discourse, equity, authenticity, leadership, and service.

Cultural transmission
is the process of passing on culturally relevant knowledge, skills, and values.

that positively transform themselves and the world around them. The hope is that once individual teachers and students understand more deeply the world to which they are connected, they will be more effective and empowered agents of change. In this way, schooling requires much more than job preparation. It is an environment for individual growth and for preparing students for global citizenship so they can navigate across social, cultural, political, and economic structures worldwide.

O'Hair, McLaughlin, and Reitzug in their teacher education textbook, *Foundations of Democratic Education*, offer a set of IDEALS for conceptualizing democratic practice in education: Inquiry, Discourse, Equity, Authenticity, Leadership, and Service. *Inquiry* refers to the need for ongoing study of individual and school practices. *Discourse* refers to the need for conversation and debate about teaching, learning, and schooling. *Equity* is the concern for achieving fair and just practices in school and society. *Authenticity* is teaching and learning that has value beyond the classroom. *Leadership* refers to the initiation of experiences that result in inquiry, discourse, and critique. *Service* is a series of experiences that develop and exhibit social responsibility. Taken together, the IDEALS are foundational for conceptualizing schools as democracies. In the next section, I apply these democratic IDEALS to the context of technology in schools.

Technology as inquiry. A democratic approach to technology and schooling frames the classroom as a microcosm of democracy where students pose problems and exchange ideas in a type of fluid, transformative dialogue. Inquiry also involves the ongoing study of one's own relationship to technology and how teaching and learning occur within mediated environments such as the classroom, the internet, and the home. Inquiry raises awareness of the language of the educators' understandings, attitudes, and associations with technology as well as with the larger environments of teaching and learning. Such **dialogic** inquiry can be supported and extended through technologies such as email, discussion boards, or blogs (see Chapter 3). The use of the internet in schools can also serve as a laboratory for public discourse and civic engagement, since the students' work is essentially public and, therefore, part of a wider forum.

Dialogic refers to the relational property of language— that language exists in response to things that have been said before and in anticipation of things that will be said in response.

Technology as discourse. A discursive approach to technology involves knowledge about and engagement in communication processes and how they in turn are shaped by technologies. Discourse also

refers to the communal conversation about technology or what occurs through the uses of communications technology. Democratic practice in schools requires educators and students to be engaged, informed, and reflective. Along with the increase in online communication comes a need for increased understanding of what is required to communicate offline or face to face. Such communication requires tolerance of immediacy, exposure, and vulnerability that is absent in online communication. Many prefer online communication as they have more "user choice" as compared to neighborhood and local community relationships. You can choose what podcast to subscribe to, but you cannot control who moves next door to you.

Technology in the service of equity. Equity in the context of technology in schools refers to achieving social justice in terms of both access to equipment as well as access to knowledge and understanding about media representations. Much of the discourse about technology in schools focuses on equipment access within impoverished communities. The National Center for Educational Evaluation in 2007 reported that although there is increased access to computers and widespread efforts to use technology to meaningfully support curricula, there is little evidence that computer technology improves teaching or learning in the current areas that bureaucratically count, namely, math and literacy. It is, therefore, troublesome that local, state, and federal government leaders continue to invest millions of dollars in computer technology, without having either evidence of educational efficacy or plans for long-term support or maintenance. Inequity emerges even across technologies. Administrators shun overhead projectors and transparencies in favor of LCD projectors and laptop computers. Meanwhile, school leaders reduce expenditures in music, art programs, and library programs.

Technology in the service of authenticity. Technology can support meaningful learning experiences and not merely the delivery of curriculum. To achieve authenticity, uses of technology must address the felt needs of a particular learning community. Unfortunately, research indicates that teachers use technology primarily for superficial "add-ons" to curriculum in contrast to their students' deeply social uses of technology. If educators position technology as a way of seeing all subject areas, then students (and teachers) can begin to understand how the processes

of teaching and learning (and living) are technologically mediated in ways that are socially, politically, economically, and culturally significant. Computers and multimedia-authoring tools allow teachers to customize learning where students can draw connections across bodies of knowledge. Technological environments that are learner-centered can more immediately address felt interests and needs of individuals and communities. Immediate and constant access to information has also erased boundaries of time and space and, therefore, increased opportunities and widened the possibilities for education and schooling.

Technology in the service of leadership. Leadership refers to the governing structures associated with technology in schools. It requires the complex navigation of technological, political, social, economic, and cultural environments of schooling. Initiation, implementation, and sustainability of educational change require knowledge of the school as a complex cultural environment. Michael Fullan writes that it's not simply a restructuring of the school environment, but a reculturing that must occur in order for change to be sustained. Technology in the service of leadership, therefore, requires systematic and systemic efforts. Although the principal is the conventional leader of the school, teachers can also provide leadership from below.

Technology in support of service learning. Service refers to the democratic practice of extending classroom learning to civic engagement outside the classroom. It extends Dewey's progressive approach of experiential learning to a wider context of social reform. From a philosophical standpoint, service implies **social reconstructionism**, alleviating social injustices within society. School is an incubator for social reformation where educators model for students and scaffold democratic practices both inside and outside the school classroom.

Social reconstructionism is an educational philosophy that emphasizes addressing social questions to create a better society.

Granted, educators face numerous challenges associated with constructing authentic, equitable, discursive, and service-oriented environments for students—let alone environments that utilize technologies in creative yet critical ways. The current bureaucratic realities of competitive high-stakes testing unfortunately detract from the educational renewal and social change that can be accomplished through a more democratic approach to technology in schools. Despite the wonders of newer technologies and our propensity to dwell in conversations about the technologies

themselves, the focus must ultimately shift away from merely accessing computer equipment and acquiring technical skills to embracing a more humanistic framework that privileges technological connections across social, political, cultural, and economic contexts.

Glossary

Technology—is a way of thinking about information, knowledge, and the world at large.

Semantics—is the study of meaning in communication.

Epistemologies—are theories of knowledge that address what constitutes knowledge, how it is acquired, and what people know.

V-chip—is a viewer control technology incorporated into television receivers that allows parents to manage or block their children's television viewing. It operates on a programming code that indicates the violence, sex, and language rating of programming.

Medium—is any channel or tool through which communication occurs.

Consumerism—equates the pursuit of happiness with the purchase of material possessions.

Multimedia—is the use of more than one medium of expression or communication.

Analog—refers to communication signals that are used in their original form. In contrast, digital communication turns analog signals into numbers that are stored on a digital device.

Audience interactivity—is the active user participation afforded by multimedia. Such interactivity implies the occurance of two-way communication.

Closed captioning—allows hearing-impaired people to access program content through text captions or subtitles that are displayed and that transcribe speech and other sounds.

Telenovela—is a popular type of Spanish soap opera.

WebTV—was a consumer technology developed in the mid-1990s that used television for display of World Wide Web content rather than a computer monitor.

World Wide Web—is a system of interlinked hypertext documents that are accessed via the internet.

Hypermedia—is an extension of hypertext where graphics, audio, video, text, and hyperlinks work together to create a nonlinear medium for communication.

Transparency—refers to the explicit understanding on the part of the user as to the ways in which technological characteristics impact communication.

PowerPoint—is a computer software program widely used in business and education as a tool for making presentations.

E-rate—is part of the federal Universal Service Fund authorized as part of the Telecommunications Act of 1996. It provides discounts to assist schools and libraries in the United States to obtain affordable telecommunications and internet access. E-rate is funded through a Universal Service fee charged to companies that provide telecommunications services.

Digital divide—is the gap between those people with access to information technology equipment (usually via computers and the internet) and the associated skills and those without access to it.

No Child Left Behind (NCLB)—is a U.S. federal law passed in 2001 that reauthorized a number of federal programs aimed at improving the performance of K-12 schooling through increasing the standards of accountability for states, school districts, and schools.

Connectivity—is the state of being connected or interconnected. It can refer to social and/or computing situations.

Media literacy—is the ability to access, analyze, evaluate, produce, and communicate using a variety of media forms.

Streaming video—refers to the delivery method of multimedia content over telecommunications networks. Video content is constantly displayed to the user while it is being delivered by the provider.

Critical pedagogy—is an approach to teaching that helps students question and challenge the dominant social and political ideologies that are ultimately oppressive.

Commodification—refers to the transformation of ideas and educational practices into commodities.

Progressivism—is an educational philosophy that emphasizes democracy, student needs, practical activities, and school-community relationships.

Civic engagement—refers to individual and collective actions that identify and address issues of public concern.

Democracy—is a process that embodies the ideals of inquiry, discourse, equity, authenticity, leadership, and service.

Cultural transmission—is the process of passing on culturally relevant knowledge, skills, and values.

Dialogic—refers to the relational property of language—that language exists in response to things that have been said before and in anticipation of things that will be said in response.

Social reconstructionism—is an educational philosophy that emphasizes addressing social questions to create a better society.

CHAPTER TWO

Shifting Perspectives

The linkage between educational success and the acquisition of technologies has a longstanding history in the United States. Technology, schooling, and commerce are inextricably interconnected. The courtship between industry and schooling heightened with the establishment of **common schools** along the midwestern frontier during the late nineteenth century. Common schools represented a nationwide effort of the U.S. government to create a cohesive body of democratic citizens as a post-Civil War influx of immigrants generated uncertainty about national unity. A widespread cultivation of citizenship required, besides other things, raising social and political awareness among immigrant settlers. This required at minimum a critical mass of literate citizens. It was then that a prominent preacher and schoolteacher named William Holmes McGuffey compiled a series of readers that featured biblical stories, literature, and folktales. *McGuffey's Eclectic Readers* imbued powerful lessons of pluralism, piety, and patriotism. The poetry and prose taught children what to believe in and how to behave by offering them tangible examples of how to enact loyalty to God, neighbor, and country. As western settlements prospered economically, the publishers downplayed

Common schools
were public schools in the United States in the nineteenth century. According to Horace Mann, common schools were meant to serve individuals of all social classes and religions.

and eventually eliminated religious content and emphasized temporal values such as hard work and consumerism. Over the course of a century, different publishers replaced original religious content with prose and poetry that celebrated industry and commerce in the United States. Although *McGuffey's* were sanitized for their religious content, the lessons of hard work and industry remained constant. To this day, *McGuffey's Eclectic Readers* remain the most successful textbooks ever published in the United States—the only exceptions being the *Bible* and *Webster's Dictionary*.

The fact that textbooks are generally costly to produce has created a chronic need among school teachers for more affordable means of instruction. In the late nineteenth century, businesses began sponsoring public school curriculum using various print formats. In 1890, a paint company donated to public school art classes a flyer explaining primary and secondary colors. Local businesses provided free instructional materials for teachers while at the same time establishing good rapport with parents who were the primary consumers during the late nineteenth and early twentieth centuries. The list of media used for business-sponsored materials evolved to include pamphlets, posters, flyers, and product samples for the school classroom. As technology advanced, so did corporate sponsorship of curriculum. Businesses donated films, videos, and more recently computer software.

With the rapid evolution of technology, the growing needs of public education, and the emergence of the adolescent as a multibillion dollar consumer market, it appears that the only real constancy during the past century of change is commerce. Derived from the Latin root *comm* (together) and *merx* (merchandise), the term denotes the buying and selling of commodities on a large scale for profit. The term commercialism has a negative connotation (particularly in the context of schooling) and refers to marketing practices that compromise quality in order to maximize profits. In its broadest sense, *commerce* denotes an exchange of ideas or opinions. In the current **information economy,** however, the lines have significantly blurred between the student as a consumer of knowledge and the student as a consumer of goods. It is, therefore, not surprising to find significant differences between adults and adolescents in terms of how they view the role of technology in schools.

Information economy
generally refers to a postindustrial economy that capitalizes on the rapid exchange and availability of information brought about most recently by the emergence of the internet and World Wide Web.

Protectionism
is a perspective based on the fear that technology can and does exert harmful influences upon users and particularly upon young people. It is enacted through filtering, censoring, or suppressing content or practices perceived as harmful, immoral, or inappropriate.

Adult Perspectives of Technology

Celebrancy

is a perspective that embodies the belief that the positive aspects of technology outweigh any potential negative effects. It assumes that technology is of ultimate benefit to education.

Cultural criticism

is a perspective that assumes technology and media institutions promote oppressive ideologies through their manipulation and representations of race, sex, and class.

Educated consumerism

is a conservative perspective that privileges the uses of technology as a vehicle for attaining economic justice. The emphasis is on acquiring information that helps one become more knowledgeable as a consumer.

Progressive era

was a period of reform in the United States between the 1890s and the 1920s that emphasized social justice and equality. It was also characterized by the belief that industry and technology could address many social problems.

When the slateboard was invented in the late 1800s, it was thought to be a major event, signaling the move from individualized instruction to group instruction. Yet the delivery model of instruction remained constant. The stimulus-response model of teaching and learning remains in existence, with the delivery of curriculum happening through the technologies of TV, computers, and the internet. What this delivery model of instruction does not acknowledge is that students do not just passively receive information but actively participate in the construction of their own learning.

The literature reveals four adult perspectives of technology: **protectionism, celebrancy, cultural criticism,** and **educated consumerism** (see Figure 1). Together, these perspectives comprise a semantic differential scale that measures two-dimensionally the moral and socioeconomic implications of technology. The vertical and horizontal axes represent respectively the perceived moral and socioeconomic implications of technology. While most adults subscribe primarily to one of the four perspectives, the stances frequently overlap depending upon the media context and situation. All four perspectives acknowledge the power of technology. However, each perspective differs as to the implications of that power.

The Celebrant Perspective

Celebrancy positions technology as providing much pleasure and hails the creative wonders (particularly of newer technologies) as solutions to many of the problems facing schools in the United States. The celebrant stance assumes that the aesthetic qualities of technology will inspire and motivate students, thus, far exceeding any potential negative effects.

The invention of the motion picture during the **progressive era** embodied celebrancy, as it presented educators with the opportunity to revolutionize classroom teaching. Thomas Edison predicted that books would one day be obsolete and that it would soon be possible to teach every branch of human knowledge with a motion picture. On an administrative level, it was thought that instructional films would lead to more efficient production of high school graduates, since more students could be taught with

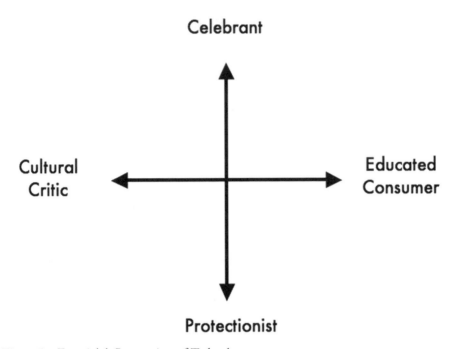

Figure 1 Four Adult Perspectives of Technology

Source: Center for Children and Technology and Media Workshop, New York

less individualized instruction from the live teacher. The debut of television at the 1939 World's Fair and its subsequent proliferation throughout homes and schools in the 1950s fed this utopian vision. Scientists and educational technologists hailed television and teaching machines as the new panaceas for education.

Celebrancy thrives on technological innovation. Teachers who subscribe to this perspective acknowledge new media and technologies simply as effective tools that aid the process of instruction and the communication of information. Many teachers and administrators embrace the "free" technology resources in an effort to reduce their out-of-pocket expenses, as many use their own funds to rent or purchase classroom supplies. A major controversy during the 1990s centered on Channel One, a 10-minute MTV-style instructional news program with two minutes of commercial advertising targeted at teens. Channel One debuted in schools in 1989 and for nearly two decades fueled the debate over commercial media and technology in schools. Students were exposed daily to advertising in exchange for TV equipment. Schools received free TVs and VCRs that educators theoretically

could use to support other school-wide activities. The celebrant discourse presented Channel One as a solution to high dropout rates, low test scores, and limited school funding. Educators, researchers, and parents praised the 12-minute commercial news program as an effective way to enliven curriculum on radically reduced school budgets. Administrators celebrated its award-winning news coverage and high production quality. Research also suggested that Channel One increased student test scores, providing supporters with tangible reasons to support its daily use in the school classroom.

Similar to Channel One, ZapMe! was introduced in schools in 1998, offering a free package of computers, software, and filtered internet access in exchange for targeted online advertising. With an audience of close to 10 million students, ZapMe! proponents said that the $100,000 package of hardware and software as well as filtered internet access was worth the minor inconvenience of advertising. The rationale was that advertising already exists on the internet and in magazines and newspapers, so why not in school? The celebrant perspective essentially ignored corporate involvement or commercial sponsorship in education, assuming the mere existence of technology in schools to have a positive impact on learning.

The emergence of the **digital age** in the 1990s compelled public discourse and policy towards thinking of computers and the internet as new panaceas for education. Teachers and students were mandated to travel on the **information superhighway** to prepare for the twenty-first century as computers became more accessible to schools across the United States. Administrators sought to build good rapport with businesses that could provide schools with the computer technology that they could otherwise not afford. The celebrant discourse frequently centered on issues of equipment acquisition, particularly computers and internet access. Of lesser priority was how teachers could use the technologies to teach students. Scholars celebrated computers, arguing that the machines enable learning to be playful, user-centered, and self-paced. Yet, minimal (if any) direction was provided to teachers to incorporate such progressive pedagogy into the classroom environment.

As mentioned in Chapter 1, it is the nonlinear, interactive, and multimedia qualities of modern communications technologies

Digital age

refers to the current time period and its emphasis on an information economy in contrast to an industrial age where the economy centers on the production of physical goods.

Information superhighway

was the terminology used to describe the internet in the early 1990s.

that present opportunities for more customizable (learner-centered) and pedagogically flexible environments for schooling. Many adults believe that the user-centered capabilities enable the current generation of students to process information and, therefore, learn differently than previous generations. Some even argue that technologies will liberate students from the traditional classroom, enabling them to be self-motivated learners and creators of their own knowledge.

A major pitfall of the celebrant perspective is that technological obsolescence blinds educators as they try to keep pace with rapid technological advancement. Such futile attempts to reconcile evolving technology and underfunding of schooling include selling hallways, classrooms, and rooftops as advertising space in exchange for equipment or funding. A celebrant perspective is also problematic as it diverts attention and resources toward equipment access and upgrades and away from the original purposes of schooling in the United States—that of basic literacy. From a celebrant perspective, schools should entertain, motivate, and inspire youth. From this standpoint, the creative and collaborative potential of technological tools outweigh any potential hazard that might be associated with commercialism.

Although privileging a celebrant perspective may spawn technology pioneers and sustain a select few who are on the cutting edge of teaching and learning with new technologies, it ultimately leaves behind a residue of uncertainty surrounding the actual costs and benefits associated with implementing and sustaining the uses of technology in schools.

The Protectionist Perspective

On the opposite end of the moral spectrum is protectionism, which is based on the fear that technology can and does exert harmful influences upon users and especially upon young people. Protectionism is enacted through filtering, censoring, or suppressing content or practices that adults perceive as harmful, immoral, or inappropriate.

Historically, efforts to protect audiences from the influence of communications technology increased significantly in the United States during the postwar 1920s when wartime **propaganda** was perceived as a threat to the nation and its schools. A 1929 Report of Committee on Propaganda in Schools organized by the

Propaganda
is a set of media messages that control what large groups of people should think.

National Education Association (NEA) defined propaganda as material conveying a single viewpoint for the purpose of controlling what students should think. The committee argued that such control contradicted the role of the teacher, whose role it was to teach students how to think, rather than what to think. Commercial posters, pamphlets, books, and radio programs were viewed as propagandistic devices to coercively influence youth. Such media, therefore, needed to be identified, controlled, and even eliminated. The widespread fear of media also spawned research about the media manipulation of audiences. The 1920s and the 1930s witnessed readership surveys, audience surveys, public opinion polls, and propaganda studies. Despite a climate of suspicion towards mass media during this time, there were no state laws or rules in a vast majority of the cities to legally protect students from being exposed to propaganda in the schools.

During the 1940s, lack of familiarity with the newer technologies in film and television fostered further suspicion of mass media transmitting propagandistic messages to vulnerable young minds. The NEA in 1946 reviewed instructional film experiments (particularly those occuring during World War II) to examine the motivational effects of film among students. Hundreds of experiments yielded tenuous results about their effects and what students learned from exposure to instructional films. Not surprising, the responsibility and burden to protect students from covert propaganda fell on the overworked classroom teacher who feared replacement by the very instructional technology in question.

Assumptions about the nefariousness of communications media and technology infected social science research during the 1950s, when researchers explored the subconscious of the human mind, which was thought to be emotional and compulsive. Vance Packard's *Hidden Persuaders* accused advertisers of using the exploitative strategy of **motivational analysis** to influence and manipulate young minds. Packard warned teachers against the use of wall charts, board cutouts, and manuals that were regularly sent to them, asserting that the primary purpose of these materials was to create child customers. In 1955, along a similar vein, the American Association of School Administrators published a guide, *Beware of Too Much Help*, warning educators of the selfish interests of businesses offering schools free curriculum materials. Such warnings

Motivational analysis was a theory that emerged in the 1950s. Critics alleged it as a conspiracy among psychiatrists, social scientists, and advertisers to manipulate the minds of young people.

attempted to inoculate students by teaching teachers how to recognize and debunk all commercial messages before they reached the student in the classroom.

The U.S. government heightened protectionist efforts in 1962 when the Federal Trade Commission concluded that the nation's children were not qualified by either age or experience to understand advertising messages. Social science research during the 1960s and the 1970s also validated fears of harmful media effects, concluding that TV violence socialized young viewers into demonstrating aggressive behaviors, shaped social attitudes, and even produced a drug-like narcotic effect among children. Activists promoted censorship of the television industry accused of producing child consumers and applied pressure through TV network protests and the raising of parental awareness. The common solutions were to shield youth from media messages either through the avoidance of the technology or through exerting pressure on media institutions to censor objectionable programming content.

Protectionism lay somewhat dormant during the economic windfall of the 1980s, as the relationship between business and education flourished in the United States. Industrial development during the second half of the twentieth century brought increased audience control through new technologies such as the television remote control and the videocassette recorder. Media audiences now had the option of censoring or avoiding commercial messages entirely. Marketers adjusted by finding other captive audience contexts to promote their messages. The 1989 debut of Channel One news programming called attention to the captive audience of students in the classroom, (re)igniting protectionist efforts to shield youth from commercialism. Protesters of Channel One argued that the two minutes of commercial advertising violated students' civil rights. Educator and activist Jonathan Kozol called Channel One nothing more than a corporate raid on education. Empirical research also validated the assumption that students purchase specific products because of the ads they see on Channel One, fuelling the protectionist belief that Channel One was both manipulative and harmful to students. Educational organizations jumped on the bandwagon to ban Channel One from classrooms. Protesting organizations included the NEA, the American Federation of Teachers (AFT), the National Parent Teacher

Association (PTA), Action for Children's Television (ACT), the National Association of Secondary School Principals (NASSP), Consumers Union Education Service (CUES), and the Center for Commercial-Free Education (also known as UNPLUG). Despite widespread protest, Channel One continued its daily broadcasts throughout the 1990s to more than 350,000 middle and high schools in the United States. After several changes in ownership and drastic declines in revenue over the past decade, Channel One reports that 8,000 schools (or 6 million students) participate in the broadcasts. Most recently, NBC News announced it would begin producing original content for Channel One broadcasts.

Protectionism also emerged in the 1990s in the forms of parental censorship of TV programs, boycotts of video games and children's toys, and a back-to-basics call to prohibit all commercial involvement in education. Organizational recommendations against commercial technology in the classroom are more prevalent than formal public policy. The NEA's "Preserve Classroom Integrity" pledge provides educators with a list of recommendations for adopting business-sponsored educational materials. NEA suggests that teachers avoid using privately sponsored curricula that promote products or that require a student to buy a product. Organizations such as the Association for Media Literacy, Center for Media Education, Center for Science in the Public Interest, Citizens for Media Literacy, and the Media Education Foundation all support an official ban on commercial media in schools.

As the use of the internet became more prevalent in schooling during the mid- to late 1990s, its unregulated, unfiltered properties generated calls for restriction and censorship. Former U.S. vice president Al Gore (although predominantly celebrant in his discourse about educational technology) acknowledged the potential harm to young people using the internet and called for policy to protect children from pornography and excessive commercialism. Kathryn Montgomery, president of the Center for Media Education (CME), lobbied for a noncommercial internet exclusively for children. Research conducted by the CME revealed that the colorful graphics and interactive games of corporate web sites seduced children into disclosing personal information. The CME also found that corporate web site advertisements for tobacco and alcohol target youth audiences. While legislation to regulate the internet continues to incubate, modern-day

protectionist efforts focus on newer technologies to save young people from the harms of those same technologies. The v-chip emerged to combat television violence; the Motion Picture Association of America (MPAA) ratings system informed movie audiences by rating film content; and software developers created internet filtering software to block user access to web sites that contain sexually explicit and/or violent content, and software that blocks pop-up ads on the internet. Ultimately, protectionism is costly, as educators incur additional expenses to shield young people from perceived harms of new technologies. This money is not well spent, as such technologies are highly inaccurate. Furthermore, protectionism does little to support media literacy, moral independence, or even social responsibility among young people. Instead, it detracts from helping young people make wise choices about technology inside or outside the school classroom.

The Cultural Critic Perspective

On the left, both literally and ideologically, is the stance of cultural critic that operates from the Marxist assumption that social power is inextricably connected to material wealth and economy. From this perspective, the technology industry and media institutions together are powerful promoters of cultural ideology through their symbolic representations of race, sex, and class. Cultural criticism is heavily grounded in the field of cultural studies and the assumption that power structures can be exposed by critically deconstructing technology practices and their associated media texts. The role of the cultural critic in this case is to specifically tease out the contradictions, discrepancies, and (mis)representations of and within media texts that may contain hidden ideologies that influence humans by their recirculation throughout society. The cultural critic stance also acknowledges schools as powerful institutions that influence cultural values.

The cultural critic stance is also represented by grassroots efforts to expose and disempower exploitative corporate alliances with schools. One argument against corporate influence in the public sphere of education is the consequent quelling of social criticism directed at business and industry. The goal of cultural criticism is ultimately activism—to bring to light harmful stereotypes and to liberate those groups that are oppressed.

Cultural criticism took hold in the United States during the 1930s, a decade rife with tension between social justice and economic growth. Progressive ideologies in the early 1900s fostered a climate of celebrating new technologies and their support of increased efficiency and productivity in schools and factories. However, the onset of economic hardship during the Great Depression ignited a public mood of activism and social reform. This mood of cultural criticism during the 1920s and the 1930s is found in the novels of Sinclair Lewis and the muckraking tactics of Upton Sinclair. The relationship between industry and schools was strained during the 1930s. Cultural criticism within education centered on the purpose of schools as sites for social criticism and change, rather than as consensus-building mechanisms. The cultural critic approach to media influence in the classroom was characterized by outrage at the perceived exploits and social injustices imposed upon schools by industry (Raup, 1936). Industrialists accused schools of being disconnected from the needs of everyday life in the 1930s and criticized schools as a luxury that very few people could and should afford.

Recommendations had been made in the 1920s to establish committees and guidelines for commercial media in schools. However, responsibility ultimately fell on the classroom teacher to help students distinguish between media concerned with social well-being and those that represented selfish motives. The Committee on Propaganda in Schools in 1929 recommended that teachers should teach students how to detect propaganda in advertisements. Many teachers rose to the call and welcomed commercial media into their classrooms as a way to train students to recognize propaganda and to develop an attitude of healthy skepticism. Armed with a critical perspective, young people were seen as empowered, rather than vulnerable.

Industry made amends with education during its efforts to stimulate the economy during and after World War II. Along with the increased spending power of youth came an increased interest in marketing to young people. Businesses widely distributed commercial materials to schools, and skeptical scholars and educators mined such materials to expose what they saw as little more than corporate propaganda disguised as curriculum. In 1979, Sheila Harty's *Huckster's In the Classroom* exposed in her classroom lessons specific examples of propaganda that were sponsored

by cereal companies, toothpaste manufacturers, cigarette manufacturers, as well as by the nuclear power, gas, auto, and meat-packing industries. Commercial industries weren't the only institutions under fire. Cultural critics also blamed the nation's educational system for catering to industry and the economic status quo, thus preventing much-needed school reform.

In the 1980s, the U.S. government instigated major cuts in public school funding, further opening school doors to commercial technologies. When Channel One debuted in classrooms in 1989, those who subscribed to cultural criticism rejected the programming on several levels. Critics charged advertisers with unfairly targeting a low-income, urban minority youth population with junk food ads. Cultural representations in the content of Channel One were arguably inaccurate. Hoynes' (1997) research revealed that blacks were represented as either athletes or prisoners; nearly three quarters of the events and issues covered were sports related; and on-camera sources were predominantly white males. Critics such as Alex Molnar and Matthew McAllister argued that Channel One dangerously confused market values with civic values and ultimately posed a threat to education, the public interest, and the common good. Such public pressure contributed to educators and policymakers banning Channel One in schools across the country, including those in New York and in some districts in California. In 1999, the United States Senate Committee on Heath, Education, Labor, and Pensions held a hearing on Channel One, during which consumer advocate Ralph Nader, media critic Mark Crispin Miller, and other research experts voiced their opposition to Channel One in schools.

Whereas protectionism seeks to censor or ban harmful technology and their content, cultural criticism seeks to stop schools from giving one company exclusive advertising rights that prohibit schools from forming other corporate partnerships and/ or prevent educators and students from speaking critically of a particular product. Although cultural criticism is justifiable in its aim to liberate oppressed social groups, the perspective over-emphasizes textual representations of media while deemphasizing the interpretive power of the audience or user. The oppressive symbolic representations of race, gender, ethnicity, and/or age tend to be the subject of critique, more than the interpretations of various audience populations. Cultural criticism of a text may

not accurately represent the audience or group it proposes to defend. Enacting cultural criticism in the classroom is also risky, as issues of social power and inequality are emotive and often volatile. In reality, classroom teachers often avoid media criticism for fear that students will get upset, that such discussions will breed cynicism, or that such analyses may not support core content curriculum.

The Educated Consumer Perspective

A more conservative and cautiously optimistic perspective of technology is educated consumerism. This perspective is literally and ideologically to the right of cultural criticism. From this perspective, technology is both the end and the means of attaining social, cultural, and economic power. The emphasis is economic (rather than social) justice, thus the educated consumer perspective privileges information that can help one become better and more knowledgeable in his/her role as a consumer. Technologies are not harmful per se but ideally require smarter choices on the part of users. Technology is merely a vehicle through which the young consumer can attain social, cultural, and economic power.

The educated consumer perspective coincides with the educational and industrial developments in the United States during the late nineteenth and early twentieth centuries when educational expansion and reform were associated with the growth of capitalistic production. In the 1920, the National Association of Manufacturers distributed to 70,000 schools a weekly gazette titled *Young America Magazine* featuring articles such as "Your Neighborhood Bank" and "The Business of America's People Is Selling." Bankers donated filmstrips and sound recording programs to schools. Educators welcomed political and financial support of schools and used such support to their educational advantage.

In the 1930s, more than half of elementary and junior high school economics teachers surveyed reported using some form of commercially sponsored material in their classrooms (i.e., posters, charts, booklets, exhibits, food samples) primarily for illustration purposes or to make class work interesting. Although teachers used commercial media, they also felt its commercial nature was more extensive than it should have been at the time. Thus, educators established criteria for selecting and using sponsored materials: currency, accuracy, and scientific basis of information. Materials

that met the criteria were used regularly and favorably by teachers as part of classroom instruction. A report sponsored by the Association of National Advertisers found the majority of advertising materials to be especially useful in home economics classrooms. Schools were more concerned with reaping the economic rewards from their relationship with industry than protecting the classroom environment from commerce. To make teacher selection of commercial classroom media more efficient, the Educators Progress Service began in 1934 the annual publication of the *Educators Guide to Free Materials*. Other industry publications soon followed from the Committee on Consumer Relations in Advertising and the Federal Works Agency.

The educated consumer stance flourished in schools during the 1940s. Special interest groups such as Junior Achievement introduced youth to commerce through entrepreneurialism. The ABC Educational Program of American Industry sponsored essay contests offering cash prizes for student essays about the history and importance of industry to the community or for student writing that outlined the history, production, and marketing of their products. In 1949, business leaders (concerned that postwar youth were ignorant about the economy) formed the National Council on Economic Education. The council worked primarily with teachers, supplying materials such as a stock market game and curricula incorporating economics into existing subject areas. In 1998, nearly half a century after its establishment, the council reported reaching 7.5 million students.

The 1962 Consumer Bill of Rights also heightened educated consumerism in the public school classroom. The bill provided Americans with the right to be informed, the right to be heard, the right to choose, and the right to safety. To better inform consumers, industry increased its supply of free product samples, displays and exhibits, maps, charts, graphs, newsletters, magazines, informational booklets, filmstrips, slides, transparencies, films and tape recordings to schools. Schools also received career education materials from the life insurance, banking, and gas industries and from the U.S. Army, FBI, and CIA. By 1965, over 90 percent of school systems in the United States permitted the use of commercial materials on the grounds that such commercial media helped students make informed decisions about their careers and consumption habits.

The 1962 Consumer Bill of Rights also spawned a consumer education movement of the 1970s. Marketing research examined where children spent their money, how often they spent, and what they bought. Consumer education was assumed to produce smarter youth consumers by teaching them critical analysis mostly of technical information about purchase transactions, the exchange process, buying a product, transfer of ownership, making monetary change, and how to distinguish among money denominations. During this time, consumer advocate Ralph Nader lobbied for a new kind of consumer education—one that integrated corporate policies and propaganda techniques along with raising public awareness about economic institutions, consumer rights, and the multiple influences of business.

In the 1980s, Americans supported reduced government spending on public schooling, thus compelling schools to depend even more on nonpublic sources of funding. Consumer research revealed that, for the first time, industry outranked parents, peers, and teachers as the number one consumer socialization agent among young people. This finding fueled both sides of the controversy surrounding Channel One in schools. From an educated consumer perspective, some considered Channel One to be of low value due to its narrow range of sources and its general lack of context, substance, and diversity in political coverage. Critics opposed the programming on the basis that requiring students to watch two minutes of commercials unnecessarily cost American taxpayers 1.8 billion dollars annually and drained 300 million dollars in public funds annually.

In 1995, consumer interest groups issued guidelines for evaluating all commercial media in schools. The Society of Consumer Affairs Professionals in Business (SOCAP) and Consumers International advocated equal standards for commercial media across curricula, suggesting that commercial media be accurate, objective, clearly written, nondiscriminatory, and noncommercial. Educated consumerism also appears in public discourse about youth and the internet. The technology of the internet allows the user to choose the level of exposure to advertising and gain more knowledge about consumer products. The Pew Internet and American Life Project reports that 87 percent of young people in the United States (ages 12–17) go online on a regular basis and nearly half of that youth population has made online purchases.

Educated consumerism, like celebrancy, endorses the technologies associated with consumerism. The stance does not favor one particular technology but rather is concerned mainly with the best value within the context of consumerism. A major problem with this perspective is that it positions young people primarily as consumers, rather than as learners. The question is not "To consume or not to consume?" but instead "What is the best value for my time and/or money?" As such, educated consumerism defines individuals according to how and what they acquire. The purpose of schools is, therefore, the production of knowledgeable consumers who will sustain the U.S. economy. A teacher may thus decide against buying a piece of edutainment software and instead buy a word-processing program because (s)he perceives basic job skills as a higher educational priority for young people. Educated consumerism does not address the social, political, and environmental implications of consuming products. As a former NEA president argued, "Children are more than little consumer units—they are living, breathing human beings with tender souls. The fierce competition of the marketplace blinds broad-casters to this all-important truth" (Geiger, 1995).

Given the history and research comprising these four adult perspectives of technology and their associated media texts, it is highly unlikely that individuals subscribe to one perspective in all cases. Rather, the context and situation determine to a large extent the quadrant in which an individual resides. For example, a teacher may subscribe primarily to a protectionist-cultural critic view of cell phones in school. However, that same teacher may subscribe to a celebrant-educated consumer perspective on computers and the internet in the classroom.

The tension that emerges from this semantic differential scale of adult perspectives of media, technology, and schooling is that they do not represent the real perspectives of young people—only the *perceived* implications of technology among young people. Although the four perspectives differ as to the nature and remedy for the effects of technology, all four perspectives assume that young people are *passive* audiences and/or users of technology. In essence, the perspectives assume a deterministic view of technology and ignore the complex meaning-making processes associated with childhood and adolescence.

Adolescent Perspectives of Technology

Decades of research reveal that adolescent youth are physiologically and psychologically different from both children and adults. During a very short time span, adolescents are confronted with establishing a sense of identity, establishing independence from parents, finishing formal schooling, formulating plans for a career or job, and learning how to establish relationships with peers. The nature of adolescent relationships shifts with the onset of puberty, as adolescents renegotiate peer relationships due to sexual attractions with one another. This is a crucial developmental period and also an effective window through which advertisers establish brand awareness and brand loyalty. In this sense, adolescence is a symbolically significant time, defined by its relationships to specific technologies, brands, and commodities. When given a choice of improving their school buildings, buying more books, hiring more teachers, or getting more computers and internet access, nearly half of young people surveyed will choose to get more computers.

Adolescent youth are also highly social beings deeply engaged in the processes of learning how to act within the culture of which they are a part. This cultural learning is both shaped and reflected by their uses of language, dress, music, and clothing, for example. Similarly, classroom learning is both shaped and reflected by adolescents' use of newspapers, magazines, television, computers, and the internet—all media technologies that supply youth with powerful symbolic materials from which to negotiate meaning and to establish an identity in the context of the world around them. Young people also actively use media and technology to construct their own identities and relationships with others. There is much research that supports the stance of young people as active interpreters and users of technologies and their associated media texts. Less clear, however, is the extent to which young people are critically aware of the institutions and strategies driving the very commercial media and technologies that target them as consumers. As adolescents, they are just beginning to develop their critical faculties—to understand abstract concepts, ideologies, and values and to develop an awareness of a larger community and common good.

When it comes to technology in schools, research suggests that young people subscribe to the perspectives of **casual acceptance, skeptical rejection, savvy consumerism,** and

Casual acceptance is an adolescent perspective that positions technology and commercialism as status quo. The assumption is that technology and schools can coexist in the right amount and combination.

Skeptical rejection is an adolescent perspective that is less optimistic and more critical of the educational value of technology. The perspective is based on negative experiences or the failure of technology to successfully support schooling.

Savvy consumerism is an adolescent perspective that privileges the consumption of technologies and their media content. The assumption is that technology is inherently educational as it supplies the user-as-consumer with essential information to make the wisest economic decisions.

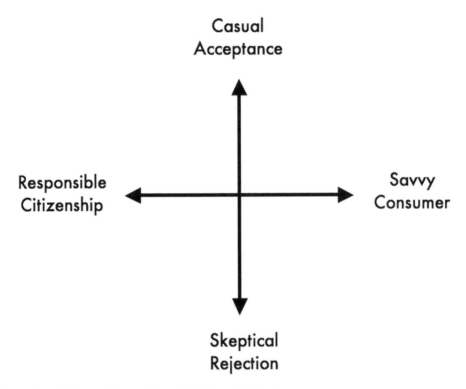

Figure 2   Adolescent Perspectives of Media and Technology

**Responsible
citizenship**

is an adolescent
perspective that relegates
the uses of technology
for civic engagement
and social responsibility
exclusively into the realm
of adulthood.

responsible citizenship (see Figure 2). Similar to the four adult perpspectives previously discussed, these four adolescent perspectives comprise a four-quadrant continuous scale in which the perspectives frequently overlap depending upon the context and situation. The vertical axis represents the perceived moral implications of technologies (to what extent they are good or bad). The horizontal axis represents adolescent understanding of the socioeconomic implications of media technology—specifically what young people do (and do not do) when using technology inside and outside the classroom.

On the top end of the spectrum is casual acceptance of technology. From this perspective, technology and its commercial nature are status quo and young people nonchalantly assume that technology and schools can coexist, in the right amount and combination. At the bottom of the spectrum is a skeptical rejection of technology, based primarily on user constraints rather than controversial content. On the extreme left (both literally and ideologically) is the concept of the responsible adult citizen who takes on civic responsibility in terms of becoming informed about current events and being civically engaged. Such engagement usually leads to the identification and navigation of unequal power structures within society. On the opposite end of the spectrum (the conservative right) is the savvy consumer perspective that positions the adolescent as economically empowered through the consumption of technologies and their associated media, yet at the same time as politically disempowered and civically disengaged.

The Casual Acceptance Perspective

From a casual acceptance perspective, technological evolution and obsolescence is status quo for young people. Instant-messaging (IM), text-messaging, and (we)blogging are the most popular uses of internet and computers among young people. Young people participate in online social networks (such as MySpace, Facebook, Xanga, an Flickr) that allow them to create profiles, message, and share multimedia content to a larger audience than is imaginable. For example, MySpace was the most visited web site of 2006, with more than 75 million users and approximately 240,000 new users added each day. Yet many young people often do not fully comprehend the consequences of posting intimate information about themselves as well as posting information that harms others. Adolescent youth use technology to further establish their identities, while at the same time claiming exemption from potentially harmful effects. Although adolescents are actively making meaning about the world around them, there is much that they do not know about media and technology, particularly when it comes to institutional forces that shape content.

The casual acceptance perspective is further reinforced by educational modes of thought that privilege technical skills (and the technology itself) over the development of critical habits of mind. The tensions between form and content can be addressed on a pedagogical level by distinguishing what Kathleen Tyner refers to as "literacies of representation" and "tool literacies." Literacies of representation include knowledge of the constructions of meaning and representation as well as the commercial media technology that shape them. In contrast, tool literacies pertain just to the technology itself. The distinction between the two types

of literacies is a significant one, as the casual acceptance perspective suggests a deficiency among adolescent youth in literacies of representation. The implications for education are significant, as schooling must make visible to students the ways in which technologies shape information.

The Skeptical Rejection Perspective

Research suggests that young people are less enthusiastic about computers as compared to their parents. They are also less optimistic about the educational value of the internet as compared to their parents. Although young people do use the internet for social purposes, more than half of them believe that the internet leads them to spend less time with their families. Other studies also suggest that young people may be sharing less with their own parents as they increasingly share a global media culture with their peers in other parts of the world. The generational gap is also expanding as a result of the "coolness factor" of technologies among young people who migrate to newer technologies and/or uses once they are adopted by their elders. Technologically nomadic behavior fuels the economy through bolstering industry and marketing. Yet, at the same time, it perpetuates the technological literacy gap between classroom teachers and their students.

It is dangerous to assume that ability to navigate digital technologies or even to participate in digital cultures implies that young people have the intellectual or moral frameworks with which to do so successfully. It is naïve to think that adolescent role playing is restricted to virtual communities and does not shape their action (and inaction) within their local real-time communities. Educators, policymakers, and parents have a responsibility to model for young people what participatory citizenship looks like in the real world. It is too easy for teachers and administrators to become complacent themselves (or let insecurities about our technical skills or a lack thereof to foster doubt and fear). It is illogical to think that democracy online equals democracy offline. Along these lines, adults need to increase their technological proficiency, not to placate the fear of being "left behind," rather to (1) interface with young people in ways that they can understand and (2) model social accountability, consequence, and moral agency. In this sense, all young people are engaged in technology apprenticeships for better or worse.

The Savvy Consumer Perspective

Consumerism is a major part of the lives of adolescent youth both inside and outside the classroom. Research reports that 66 percent of teens online use the internet to research a purchase or a new product and 31 percent use the internet to buy a product. Savvy consumerism embodies the wealth of experience young people have as consumers of technologies and their media content. Technology is inherently educational as it supplies the student-as-consumer with essential information that young people and educators believe will allow them to make the best economic decisions about what to buy and where to buy. A major problem with the savvy consumer perspective is that although (at best) it teaches students to be responsible and caring consumers, it primarily positions them as consumers rather than as citizens. A recent example is the popular social networking site Facebook, which was sharply criticized in 2007 for violating users' privacy by tracking online purchasing activity and then posting it online. In protest, at least 10,000 Facebook subscribers signed a petition to curb what many perceived as unfair marketing practices. Eventually, Facebook reconfigured the site to allow subscribers the choice of sharing or keeping private their internet activity. Critics complain that opting out is not user-friendly and even difficult to configure within the Facebook user preferences. This example points to the ultimate goal of savvy consumerism, which is to serve consumerism itself. Ultimately, savvy consumerism requires no obligation to the world or even to other consumers. One purpose of schooling is to, therefore, balance students' excessive consumer and social uses of media and technology with democratic practices that require responsible stewardship of local and global communities.

The Responsible Citizen Perspective

Responsible citizenship carries with it the obligation to care about the world and its people. It is a much more elusive and unpopular perspective among adolescent youth as compared to the other three perspectives. Arguably it is much easier, interesting, and basic for young people to actively accept technology in the classroom rather than to criticize the global consequences of technological development and consumerism. However, students relegate this perspective, and any associated responsibilities, to adulthood. One of the hazards of adolescence is that it allows

young people to claim exemption from the vulnerability associated with childhood while at the same time exempting themselves from the social responsibilities associated with adulthood. Recent data from the Center for Information and Research on Civic Learning and Engagement (CIRCLE) show a serious decline in civic engagement among young people, with more than half of 15–25-year-olds completely disengaged from civic life. Adolescents can leverage technology to this end. David Buckingham argues that the social construction of childhood not only alienates young people from the adult world, it ultimately positions them to be noncitizens. He found in his research that when children argued explicitly for the need for parental regulation of media use, they did so only with regard to children much younger than themselves. Among older age groups, most children asserted that they were mature enough to make their own decisions about what they should watch and to take the consequences. Since adolescents are not children, however, it follows that they should participate to a certain extent in the adult world. It also follows that schools are at least partially responsible for preparing young people to participate as adults in the wider social and political structures.

Reconciling the Differences

The schema of four adolescent perspectives serves as a cross-disciplinary continuum for educators as they use (or prepare to use) technology in the classroom. It provides a continuum through which educators can gauge students' perspectives and assist them in moving toward a more democratic perspective of and through their uses of technology. Such identification of perspectives is essential to constructivist-based pedagogy, especially when cultivating civic responsibility among students. Entrance into the larger adult world also requires a shift in perspective from one that is consumer-centered to a more creative perspective that is socially and politically responsible. Classroom uses of technology can initiate a larger dialogue in which students have a voice and actively participate.

The implication of adolescent development upon schooling is significant. If educators are to follow the traditional democratic purpose of participatory citizenship, then it follows that teachers as adults must cultivate the critical faculties of young people as their students, particularly when it comes to technology. This requires that

teachers temper excessive protectionism (on the part of the administration) with a balance of educated consumerism and cultural criticism. Since young people are already well versed in casual acceptance and savvy consumerism, teachers can mine these perspectives for pedagogical insight and for ways in which to move students along the continuum toward responsible citizenship. In this sense, schooling is an important institutional mechanism with the potential of harnessing the critical capabilities of young people, as they interact with a diverse population and a variety of technologies. The challenge lies in the differences between teachers and students. Today's students may be what Marc Prensky refers to as **digital natives** who have established relationships with technology since infancy and think and process information differently than their predecessors. In contrast, Prensky identifies their teachers as **digital immigrants** who may adopt the use of new technologies but frequently revert to past practices and skills that are foreign to their students. At the same time, while students may possess more advanced technological skills than their teachers, their abilities to critically reflect upon the technologies and their associated media texts are less established. As teachers become more fluent in their uses of technology (particularly in the classroom), they are more able to focus on cultivating critical thinking and decision making among young people.

> **Digital native**
>
> refers to a person who has grown up with digital technologies.

> **Digital immigrant**
>
> refers to a person who grew up without digital technologies but adopted their use later on in life.

Glossary

Common schools—were public schools in the United States in the nineteenth century. According to Horace Mann, common schools were meant to serve individuals of all social classes and religions.

Information economy—generally refers to a postindustrial economy that capitalizes on the rapid exchange and availability of information brought about most recently by the emergence of the internet and World Wide Web.

Protectionism— is a perspective based on the fear that technology can and does exert harmful influences upon users and particularly upon young people. It is enacted through filtering, censoring, or suppressing content or practices perceived as harmful, immoral, or inappropriate.

Celebrancy—is a perspective that embodies the belief that the positive aspects of technology outweigh any potential negative effects. It assumes that technology is of ultimate benefit to education.

Cultural criticism—is a perspective that assumes technology and media institutions promote oppressive ideologies through their manipulation and representations of race, sex, and class.

Educated consumerism—is a conservative perspective that privileges the uses of technology as a vehicle for attaining economic justice. The emphasis is on acquiring information that helps one become more knowledgeable as a consumer.

Progressive era—was a period of reform in the United States between the 1890s and the 1920s that emphasized social justice and equality. It was also characterized by the belief that industry and technology could address many social problems.

Digital age—refers to the current time period and its emphasis on an information economy in contrast to an industrial age where the economy centers on the production of physical goods.

Information superhighway—was the terminology used to describe the internet in the early 1990s.

Propaganda—is a set of media messages that control what large groups of people should think.

Motivational analysis—was a theory that emerged in the 1950s. Critics alleged it as a conspiracy among psychiatrists, social scientists, and advertisers to manipulate the minds of young people.

Casual acceptance—is an adolescent perspective that positions technology and commercialism as status quo. The assumption is that technology and schools can coexist in the right amount and combination.

Skeptical rejection—is an adolescent perspective that is less optimistic and more critical of the educational value of technology. The perspective is based on negative experiences or the failure of technology to successfully support schooling.

Savvy consumerism—is an adolescent perspective that privileges the consumption of technologies and their media content. The assumption is that technology is inherently educational as it supplies the user-as-consumer with essential information to make the wisest economic decisions.

Responsible citizenship—is an adolescent perspective that relegates the uses of technology for civic engagement and social responsibility exclusively into the realm of adulthood.

Digital native—refers to a person who has grown up with digital technologies.

Digital immigrant—refers to a person who grew up without digital technologies but adopted their use later on in life.

CHAPTER THREE

Pedagogical Stages

Although the United States is founded on democratic principles, our civilization is fundamentally a technological one. The rapid technological development over the past two centuries has been stupendous. The years between 1850 and 2000 yielded the typewriter, telephone, ball point pen, phonograph, photography, motion pictures, radio, television, personal computer, word processor, audio and video cassette recorders, videodisc, compact disc, video games, mobile phones, cellular phones, the internet, Post-It notes, and the laser printer. Film cameras evolved into disposable cameras, digital cameras, and camera phones. Analog television morphed into high-definition (HDTV) digital format and converged with WebTV. The CD-ROM begat the DVD and the videocassette recorder evolved into the digital video recorder. And the technological advancement and media convergence continue at an astounding rate. Just when educators gain a foothold on technology, the landscape shifts right under our feet. For every teacher who responds rapturously to a new technology, there are at least four others who lament the mechanization and commodification of education. This love-hate relationship between teachers and technology is not surprising given that historically

the ones who produced, promoted, and positioned technology in schools and classrooms were technicians, not teachers.

Arguably one of the most controversial and influential communications technology to date is the internet. Many consider it to be a fairly recent phenomenon, yet it has existed for more than 40 years, originating in the early 1960s as a means of securing data through the United States Defense Department ARPANET (Advanced Research Projects Agency Network). By 1985, the internet was an established technology supporting computer science researchers and developers. Over the past two decades, the population of internet users in North America has reached approximately 70 percent. Wireless computer networks literally the size of small countries now provide humans with constant connectivity to information and to one another. In its second generation, often referred to as **Web 2.0**, users can access multimedia software applications on the Web and on demand. In one sense, this evolutionary functionality of the World Wide Web levels the playing field as users need only a computer terminal and high-speed access to the internet.

When it comes to public education and schooling, however, widespread access to multimedia or **rich media** comes at a substantial cost. Under the old twentieth-century network standard, only a few teachers and students could simultaneously log onto the internet and partake of the layers of video, audio, and data content, given that such access requires large bandwidth. Since the year 2000, school administrators and technology coordinators have upgraded and upscaled their web technology by going high-speed and wireless, allowing exponentially more students, teachers, parents, and administrators to log on at the same time. Between 2001 and 2005, the percentage of public schools using wireless networks increased from 10 percent to 45 percent. While going wireless is less expensive than wiring buildings (particularly in rural areas), it is not yet a widespread practice in schooling in the United States.

A new digital divide has emerged in the realm of high-speed networks. A 2006 study of the National Science Foundation reports that although nearly all U.S. schools have internet access, only about half of the student population accesses the internet while at school. Young people also perceive a strong disconnect between how they use the internet at home and how they use it

Web 2.0

refers to the second generation of the World Wide Web and is characterized by applications and data residing on the web.

Rich media

refers to advanced technology that allows for media interactivity (combining text, audio, and video) as well as interactive experiences on the part of the user.

Pedagogy

the art and science of teaching. The term also refers to strategies or styles of teaching.

and do not use it with teachers at school. A common pitfall among teachers is their reliance on traditional **pedagogy** that emphasizes the delivery of information rather than knowledge transformation. Teaching with and about technology is much more complex than the educational climate suggests. Meaningful uses of technology require an integrated knowledge of content, pedagogy, and technology and how they work together to comprise learning environments. Such exploration of new terrain requires focused and sustained professional development—rarely utilized or even offered to teachers. Instead, teachers are literally left to their own devices. Conversation and debate that should focus on curriculum and pedagogy default to debates or complaints about the technology itself. When it comes to technology in schools, the important question among educators should be: "How does learning occur?" The remainder of this chapter offers educators a roadmap to understanding technology and learning through four stages of pedagogical development.

Stages of Pedagogical Development

Hierarchy of needs

is a psychological theory set forth by Abraham Maslow in 1943. It is usually depicted as a pyramid consisting of five levels: Physiological, safety, love/belonging, esteem, and self-actualization. The first four levels are characterized as physiological and the top level is associated with psychological needs.

The pedagogical uses of technology in schools can be thought of as a hierarchical pyramid similar to the **hierarchy of needs** proposed by well-known psychologist Abraham Maslow. In Maslow's hierarchy, the assumption is that the basic or first level(s) of need must be satisfied in order for higher levels of need to be satisfied. With pedagogical development, there are at least four levels of technology use that comprise the hierarchy: Content management, authoring, collaboration, and cultural transformation (See Figure 3). The assumption is that the higher, more complex levels of pedagogy can be achieved only after the lower, more basic levels are achieved.

Stage One: Content Management

The first stage follows the traditional cultural transmission model of schooling and is found in the pervasive language of instructional or content delivery. The epistemology that dominates the field of educational technology is logical positivism—the assumption that objective facts comprise reality and that these facts can be perceived by humans. The logical positivist approach

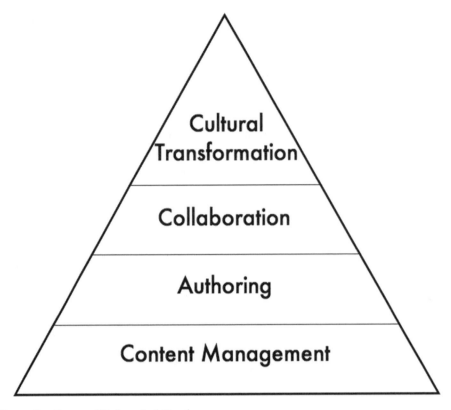

Figure 3   Stages of Pedagogical Development

to knowledge positions the knower separate from the known. Thus humans merely need to search for knowledge that already exists. The dominant strategy is, therefore, to find ways of accessing information. Conversely, new technologies afford ways for teachers to assess student retention of information. Audience response systems work with hand-held devices to allow students to key in their responses (i.e., multiple-choice, true/false, yes/no) and beam them wirelessly to a computer that converts them into data that teachers can use to inform their instruction.

Accessing information—particularly via the internet—has generated a wake-up call for educators in the area of student cheating and plagiarism. It is easier than ever to copy electronic information and download prewritten papers available online. According to Lathrop and Foss (2000), 80 percent of high school students admit to cheating and 95 percent of students who cheat say they do not get caught. Cell phones have also created an easy avenue for cheating, as students can capture digital photos of

exams and text-message answers to one another. Yet banning cell phones from classrooms may be misguided, as educators can leverage the ubiquity of cell phone technology to teach students how to use them in ways that are both ethical and academic.

The technological epitome of content management is courseware (a hybrid of *course* and *software*). Courseware is a content (or data) management system applied to education. It is popular in higher education and is rising in popularity in K-12 education. Common examples include Blackboard, WebCT, Pipeline, and the **open source** version Moodle. Courseware features vary but commonly include a container for course materials, email, **discussion board,** a virtual classroom (chat), a grade book, and a student workplace. For colleges and schools, courseware is an efficient means for automating course enrollments and managing student data. It also affords students and families access to course content from anywhere and at anytime. Such access is contingent upon reliable, high-speed internet connection and compatible hardware and software. In higher education, courseware is essentially an online template that can support increased communication between teachers, students, and their families. The student can transfer information (i.e., papers, assignments, projects) to and from the course container. An online grade book feature allows the teacher to transmit back to the student (and parents) both quantitative and qualitative assessments. This two-way transmission of information is, to a certain extent, useful and efficient as it can occur outside the boundaries of time and space, increasing the flexibility and convenience for students. However, since it is based on transmission or delivery of information, it is limited when it comes to enhancing the quality of teaching and learning.

Some teachers use discussion boards within courseware environments to generate communal dialogue. However, the results are often static. Within Blackboard courseware, for example, the discussion forum feature consists of forums and threads. The course administrator (teacher) creates a forum by posting a topic or a question that serves as an impetus for subsequent threads, or postings from students (e.g., "To what extent do you think the characters from Chapter Two are realistic?"). Course participants respond accordingly in **asynchronous mode**. Although the intention might be to initiate authentic, meaningful conversation,

Open source

is a set of principles and practices on how to write software, the source code for which is openly available.

Discussion boards

are internet communities for holding discussions and posting user-generated content.

Asynchronous mode

refers to communication that is not existing or happening at the same time.

what emerges is a manufactured discourse within a constrained hierarchy of threads. Courseware may provide an inlet for participants to contribute. However, students cannot create their own forums unless the teacher designates the students as co-administrators of the course. Thus, the teacher maintains ultimate control of communication. Some teachers may require discussion board participation from their students, increasing the pressure on students to manufacture discourse. Discussion board threads frequently resemble a collection of responses governed by the teacher's original prompt, rather than a transformative dialogue. Students confuse posting the most (quantity) with meaningful discussion (quality). A discussion board might resemble what the teacher wants to hear rather than a site that is authentic and layered and having deeper meaning than the sum of its individual threads.

Ultimately, courseware is a useful administrative tool for managing data—be it providing course content or tracking student participation. Pedagogical innovation, however, is left entirely in the hands of the teacher. Without professional development that emphasizes theories of learning with technology, the best-intentioned teachers revert to a digital chalk-and-talk that merely transplants course content into an online environment. The students most likely to benefit from digital access to course content are those who are already successful managers of information. Similarly, the teachers who will most likely benefit from courseware are those who can already manage data in high volume. Courseware also requires significantly more preparation time than traditional, face-to-face instruction and can significantly increase a teacher's weekly workload from seven hours to 20 hours! So, while courseware may afford efficient management of large amounts of data (such as student enrollments), it requires from teachers a large investment of time, effort, and money for a questionable pedagogical return.

The ease and flexibility of content management significantly increases, however, with portable devices, such as web-enabled cell phones, iPods, mp3 players, and the personal digital assistant (PDA). The PDA began as a pocket organizer and has evolved into a mobile tool for teachers and students. It provides a calendar, some games, a music player, and email and internet access. However, it can now also support video recording, word processing,

Global Positioning System (GPS)

is a global navigation satellite system that enables a GPS receiver to determine its location, speed, direction, and time.

database design, and **global positioning system** (GPS) access. With any of these devices, students can easily access, download, and transport primary source documents, photographs, film records, newspaper archives, and even advice from experts. Students can then access courseware from many different locations and manage different types of content: Take notes, record teacher lectures, track homework assignments, keep a school calendar, and transfer files in between school and home. Thus, student exposure to and interaction with the new mobile technologies can increase students' information management skills. A notable example is a K-12 partnership between schools in New York and a team of scientists at Clarkson University. While the scientists traveled to Antarctica to study how sea ice responds to forces of nature, students in New York stayed connected through the internet via interviews with scientists, photos, and research updates.

It should be noted that (increased) access to content is a prerequisite to content management. For example, e-books (electronic books) can assist struggling readers and students with disabilities by supplying them with access to texts that were previously inaccessible.

Stage Two: Authoring

Once teachers and students acquire basic skills of managing media content, they can then focus on being authors of multimedia. Authorship is central to achieving technological and media literacies. In the digital world, authoring tools include multimedia presentations, web publishing, and digital video production, all of which provide students with rich opportunities for telling stories about themselves, what they learn, and how they apply knowledge to the world around them. Common software applications such as PowerPoint, Hyperstudio, SuperCard, Director, iMovie, Moviemaker, and iDVD have allowed users to create their own multimedia content locally on their desktops without using the internet or the web. By combining (hyper)text, graphics, images, and video, students can richly describe their experiences and knowledge. For example, students can express their understanding of the Periodic Table of Elements, dinosaurs, or the works of Edgar Allan Poe by strategically integrating text, audio, images, and graphics to produce a multimedia artifact that conveys meaning in multidimensional ways. Along more socially and

YouTube

is a video-sharing web site created in 2005 where users can upload, view, and share video clips. In July 2006, 100 million videos were being watched everyday.

TeacherTube

is an online community for uploading, viewing, and sharing instructional videos related to student learning and teacher professional development.

SchoolTube

is a media-sharing website for teachers and students in K-12 schools. The site is moderated and requires that all student created content follow local school guidelines and be approved by registered teachers before it is made available on the Web.

Social networking sites

are online communities of people who share interests and activities. They provide various ways for users to interact, such as messaging, email, video, file sharing, blogging, and discussion groups.

historically conscious lines, one teacher had his high school students assemble photographs of the 1950s bus boycotts and compare them to photographs of the 1960s freedom rides, generating critical discussions about the differences between the two events.

With increased internet bandwidth and speed, users of all ages can communicate and distribute their work to a worldwide audience. **YouTube** (http://www.youtube.com) is a popular example of individual users acting as both producers and distributors of original multimedia content. Other sites such as MySpace, Yahoo, Google, and MSN also feature user-generated videos. On the educational side is **TeacherTube** (http://www. teachertube.com), a site that allows educators to upload and to access user-generated instructional videos. Similarly, **SchoolTube** (http://www.schooltube.com) emphasizes student-produced media. Recently, companies have built **social networking sites** for K-12 schools that address several important educational needs: (1) Increasing awareness of internet safety; (2) Acquiring technology-related skills; (3) Moving beyond the notion of the internet as an online library; and (4) Using the internet in school to support online publishing and communication. The purposes of educational social networking sites are to allow students to comment on and view other students' work (e.g., writing, art portfolios) in a contained environment that is monitored by the teacher. The school or district, as compared to the uncontrolled and primarily commercial environment of popular social networking sites, can administer the network.

iPodagogy and Podcasting. Global multimedia distribution is also the basis of the current phenomenon of podcasting (or web casting) that consists of a simple RSS (Really Simple Syndicate) software program and an aggregator that allows any user to author an audio and/or video web cast. Other users can subscribe to the RSS feed and when the author publishes a new file online, it is automatically delivered to the subscriber's computer (similar in concept to the regular home delivery of a newspaper). The file can then be downloaded to a portable device for increased portability and student mobility. Users can share their podcasts through social bookmarking, allowing teachers and students to pass on material to future classes. Students can create a customized school internet portal. They can subscribe to podcasts from their teachers and

from whomever else—the principal, for example. Parents too can subscribe to podcasts. There are thousands of podcasts worldwide from which teachers and students can choose. David Warlick's Education Podcast Network (http://www.epnweb.org/) features hundreds of selections from elementary, middle, and secondary schools across the world. Students in Great Britain record music on donated iPods during music class to listen and learn about pentatonic scales and to then vocally record their music commentaries. They also download paintings to view for art class. In Australia, elementary school students create podcasts on bullying. In California, East Oakland Community High School ("Education Not Incarceration") touts an award-winning podcast, "This East Oakland Life" (http://eastoakland.libsyn.com/). Students write and broadcast stories about french fries, drugs, prostitution, love, and cutting school. The British Broadcasting Corporation (BBC) describes the podcast as "a window into a community with problems the mainstream media often overlooks, but it's also a demonstration of how new technology can help to give young people a voice."

Podcasting has dramatically increased the scope and frequency of an author's audience. A recent forecast from eMarketer predicts that the total U.S. audience for podcasts could reach 50 million by 2010. The public response to podcasting is so strong that *The Oxford American Dictionary* named *podcast* the "Word of 2005." The neologism **ipodagogy** emerged in response to the increased uses of iPods and podcasting for teaching and learning in education. Campbell (2005) points out that the power of podcasting lies in:

> the delicate, responsive human interaction that characterizes the best communication, indeed the best *listening* and *reading*…There is magic in the human voice, the magic of shared awareness. Consciousness is most persuasively and intimately communicated via voice. (p. 40)

While teachers creating podcasts of their lectures or homework assignments for students to download on a regular basis may increase efficiency, such uses resemble content management (Stage One). More advanced uses of ipodagogy cater to a **liberatory pedagogy** of both teachers and students (as authors) sharing their multimedia creations to a worldwide audience. The capability of podcasting

---

iPodagogy

is the study of teaching methods using iPods or other handheld audio and/or video devices.

Liberatory pedagogy

is the practice of education for liberation or critical pedagogy. It incorporates a struggle for meaning as well as a struggle for freedom and justice.

and portable devices, such as iPods, to support print literacy and the struggle of non-English-speaking students is a boon to educators in the United States. Similarly, using iPods can bridge classroom learning with what students do at home. English Language Learner (ELL) students at a Nebraska middle school use a voice recorder with the iPod to record English and Spanish, then import the audio files into slideshow presentations so that their Spanish-speaking parents could understand their work. Another teacher uses a video iPod to visually sign assignments and vocabulary words for deaf students, including captions to add meaning.

What makes podcasting ideal for education is that it is low-tech, inexpensive, and accessible to the masses. *Our Media: The Global Home for Grassroots Media* (http://www.ourmedia.org) is one example of using open source software to host video, audio, images, and text. The site offers users unlimited bandwidth, so students and teachers can host blogs and publish podcasts free of charge. However, technical proficiency is essential if a podcast is to reach a wide audience, including those who are without high-speed internet connections. A podcast file with a higher sampling rate, greater bit depth, and higher compression bit rate will produce a large file size, requiring large bandwidth—which is neither infinite nor accessible to all.

Ultimately, iPodagogy is commercially driven. The other side of the student-as-author equation is student-as-consumer. It is significant that Apple Computer integrates its podcasting and iTunes software, so that users are immediately led to the iTunes Music Store to purchase content. On the other hand, administrators often choose inexpensive PCs (rather than the Macintosh operating system) based on pricing alone. They often do not consider that Macintosh computers arrive fully equipped with a variety of multimedia-authoring software whereas PCs do not. It is significant that the bottom line for the technology industry is to sell more devices, not necessarily educate more children.

Educators must critically evaluate the ways in which they provide the technological infrastructure for students to be productive and safe technology users and authors of multimedia. Educators must also consider that a student's media consumption outside of school may collide with classroom norms and school policies. Recently, a teacher in Philadelphia was assaulted by two of his

students when he confiscated an iPod during class. The teacher was hospitalized for broken vertebrae and the students were expelled and charged with assault. Given the social, political, and economic meanings surrounding these technologies in schools, educators must determine what levels of consumerism are acceptable in achieving technological literacy. There is an abundance of other digital, electronic, print, and object media that support authorship (including the classic duo of pen and paper).

Stage Three: Collaboration

The educational power of Web 2.0 lies in user-generated content and the circulation of that content. Stage Three focuses on students working together to author content. Innovative software and access to the Web afford students access to data so they can then manipulate those data and co-create new knowledge. Recently, Google donated to K-12 teachers online software that automatically stores data on Google's servers, rather than on the user's computer. Google provides an online guide for teachers on how to incorporate the software applications into their curriculum. The ubiquity of the software has tremendous power to reshape the dynamics of teaching and learning in schools. Students in different locations can collaborate by viewing and editing documents simultaneously. For better or worse, teachers can access students' papers before they submit them. The assumption is that knowledge is transformed more rapidly and therein lies the potential for achieving deeper understanding and a deeper level of collaboration in the context of school. A 2007 study conducted by the National School Boards Association revealed that 96 percent of students between the ages of 9 and 17 who have online access use social networking sites, such as MySpace. The study also revealed that 50 percent of those students talk specifically about homework and 60 percent discuss education-related topics such as college or career planning, learning outside of school. The potential of Web 2.0 technologies (i.e., social networking, weblogging) lies in students creating their own educational environments as they connect with others and form online communities of learning:

> This involvement is not a singular act; rather an active and
> collective process of learning. Within these social settings, young

> people create and develop their own perspectives and knowledge. Participation provided young people a context and community to explore imaginations and ideas. This process of learning, situating educational activity in the lived experience of young people, is dialogical and open-ended. The various media become more than facilitators and instruments; they enable and mediate learning and literacy. They become 'social networks' of learning. (Asthana, 2006, p. 8)

This social networking and online collaboration is not entirely new, however. More than a decade ago, scholars asserted the significance of computer-mediated environments such as online communities and multiuser dungeons in the construction of identity, knowledge, and community. More recently, a new literacy has emerged: *Network literacy* is the ability to write in a collaborative environment and support learning and teaching with emergent technologies. But only within recent years have corporations and educators successfully lobbied such literacies as curriculum standards.

The current generation of the internet and World Wide Web is a context for creation and not just an information source for research. The epitome of this is a blog (web + log), also known as an online journal that can be commented on by others. Blogging is characterized by a stream-of-consciousness and a social or political commentary style of writing. Any individual with internet access and an email address can establish a blog and express their ideas on the web. A teacher can use a blog similar to an online bulletin board to review what happened in class and to assign homework. Relatives can log in from anywhere around the world and view their work. Blogging has a high degree of potential for supporting communication and collaboration within and across school settings—to connect staff with students and students with other students. Collaborative uses of blogs include students commenting on classmates' work. One elementary school in Maryland requires students to keep reading response journals as the foundation for classroom blogs and to create collaborative blogs with students from other grades. Junior high school students in Missouri recently blogged about a historical novel along with its author in Pennsylvania. The project expanded to include students at a middle school in California. The students asked the author questions and the author responded directly to the students'

inquiries, posted her own questions, and recorded a podcast for students.

Blogging is not necessarily about social networking. Rather, blogging affords the communal creation of course content through a type of structured social interfacing. Although blogging does provide an outlet for reticent students to participate, in addition to getting students interested in writing, there are also pitfalls associated with blogging. A major challenge is how to bridge student enthusiasm and skill for writing in a social context with the standards and expectations of writing in an academic environment. Major differences include expressing opinion versus conveying facts or citing credible sources. Conducting research and conveying information in an original way are also requisites for academic writing. Additional challenges of blogging relate to student conduct such as bullying or "flaming" that may result in the use of language inappropriate to an academic setting or lead to even more serious illegal behavior. Some teachers require students to sign a code of conduct and involve even parents in the process by requiring them to review assignment guidelines and by expecting them to grant their child written permission to participate in activities involving the internet. Another teaching strategy is to model for students what is considered appropriate blog postings and collectively discuss how to post comments that are pertinent, civil, and respectful.

On pedagogical and professional levels, blogging can also support and extend traditional professional development for teachers, as an extension of a one-day workshop. Teachers can communally participate as **cybercitizens** to engage more deeply (both synchronously and asynchronously) in issues related to teaching, learning, and technology—and in ways that accommodate their own learning styles, professional schedules, and personal lives. Blogging provides a mechanism for teacher observations, evaluations, understandings, and epiphanies. Blogging illuminates collective understanding and helps teachers to indirectly answer their own questions through dialogue. Authentic online collaboration is difficult to achieve, however. Students are inclined to socially network via the internet as individuals more than they are willing to civically engage in more traditional communal ways. There is concern that the uses of newer digital technologies and virtual spaces distract from the

Cybercitizen
is a person who is actively involved in online communities and uses the internet to engage in activities that are socially and/or politically responsible.

traditional forms of social engagement and real world lived experiences—altering the nature of community and communal interaction.

Wikis are an extension of blogging in the sense that they are communal and collaborative web sites that allow multiple authors to create and edit information on the site. Wikipedia (http://www.wikipedia.org) is a popular online encyclopedia created by a common collective. It allows anyone to post and edit information and provides multiple viewpoints on approximately 750,000 entries. However, it is more than an encyclopedia as it facilitates peer interaction and shared knowledge among learners. It is a representation of online collaboration, communal dialogue, and critical debate. The content is ever evolving (by anyone and anonymously) and, therefore, needs to be kept in check through other, more authoritative, sources. This triangulation of research that involves source corroboration is a necessary process to achieving information literacy. Although some teachers have criticized students' overreliance on the popular internet encyclopedia Wikipedia, some college professors instead require their students to write Wikipedia entries in lieu of term papers.

Students can work collaboratively to create a wiki within a particular area of interest or to study or even solve a problem. If students are studying a country, city, community, or neighborhood, they can participate in a free online global project titled *WikiPlaces: The Essence of Your Favorite Places* (http://wikiplaces.wetpaint.com) that is open to all ages. Participants communicate "the essence of a place" by creating an alphabet book page for that place. Contributors can add links, video, and images and customize formatting. By viewing the page history, students can see who has made edits to the page. Ultimately, what blogs and wikis provide is an efficient, low-cost means of group collaboration without the burden of sharing computer platforms, software, or even documents. What is often downplayed, however, is the necessary print literacy (reading and writing) required to effectively incorporate these technologies into education. It is unclear whether young people are able to shift easily from one form of communication to another.

Web 2.0 technologies can support a professional development community of teachers. An online community can be designed initially as a work and meeting space for teachers, and as a means of collecting data to inform curriculum development. An online portal can provide a team of teachers with the ability to share knowledge/files through online discussions as well as to access commonly used applications and databases such as Google Documents, Blogger, Wikipedia, and TeacherTube. Teachers can also collectively create a wiki that identifies, documents, defines, and maps bodies of curriculum standards relevant to technological literacy among students and teachers (i.e., American Library Association, ISTE National Educational Technology Standards). It also supports thinking about information in deeper and more discerning ways as opposed to merely sharing information in a social setting. While blogging is democratic in its design (privileging the voice of individuals), incorporating blogging as part of the academic curriculum requires some bureaucratic retooling. How do students engage in "smart" conversation about subject matter with their peers? How are blogs assessed? Are students required to prove their comprehension of subject matter? Are students evaluated on their ability to make connections across ideas? Should students use proper spelling and grammar in their blogs? While each of these technologies provides opportunities for increased collaboration and community among students and teachers, they also require teachers to surrender the privacy of what they do within the four walls of the classroom to a global audience. In addition, if a significant amount of access, authorship, reflection, and collaboration can occur online, then what becomes the purpose of the face-to-face classroom?

Stage Four: Cultural Transformation

At the top of the pedagogical hierarchy is a level of creativity and complexity that involves a multiplicity of transactions among student, teacher, technology, and curriculum. Through Stages One through Three, students (and teachers) are already skillful managers, authors, and collaborators of multimedia content. They are empowered agents of change, as they have achieved a level of technological transparency that enables them to concentrate their efforts on transforming the local communities in which they live. At this level, the goal is to leverage technology to change those aspects of social and political institutions that are

problematic and even oppressive. For example, in 2006, the Los Angeles Unified School District in California began its Diploma Project, using a text-messaging campaign, FM radio spots, and advertisements on MySpace and Facebook to keep at-risk students in school and to reenroll those who had already left. Virtual schools (that offer regular school courses in distance-education formats) allow students to earn their high school diplomas in circumstances they might not otherwise in a traditional face-to-face setting. Teen pregnancy, threat of gang involvement, physical disabilities, disciplinary problems, and/or homeschooling are just some of the reasons that virtual schooling is popular. However, its effectiveness in terms of learning is questionable, particularly since the dropout and failure rates are reportedly 60 to 70 percent.

The United Nations Educational, Scientific and Cultural Organization (UNESCO) recently asserted that young people are protagonists who are "capable of making decision, exercising choices…and who are active agents in promoting democratic processes and civic engagement" (Asthana, 2006, p. 7). Across the world in North India, a Mapping the Neighbourhood Project involves school children from the rural and urban regions using PDAs and GPS technologies to visually construct a map of the places in the community. School children have an opportunity to learn about their regional geography and share it with other members of the community. A notable characteristic of this project is the connections forged between the students and the members of the rural communities as they engage in community development—training in citizenship. Since no village maps existed, the students

> collected and marked GPS locations of all water resource points (natural and manmade). The location of each house was marked and liked to GIS in order to be able to reassess the water need and supply situation. Other built structures (temples, roads and pathways, shops, community center, health centers, other infrastructures etc.) were also mapped. (Asthana, 2006, p. 53)

The educational value of this mapping project extends beyond schooling, in forging connections as students engage directly in community development. Similarly, in New Orleans, Louisiana (USA), Alan Gutierrez of the Think

New Orleans project (http://www.thinknola.com) coordinates a Neighborhood Mapping Project as part of the post-hurricane reconstruction of the city.

The "Rock Our World" project (www.rockourworld.org) is a global collaborative project of Carol Anne McGuire, an elementary school teacher of the blind and visually impaired. Using music-editing software, web cams, and internet chat, she recruited teachers from eight classrooms on six continents to help their students create one track of music. On a weekly basis, each class would email the music track to another team, who would them add their new track to the file and then forward it on to the next class. When the track returned to the original school, students saw how their original track was modified. McGuire wanted music to build bridges between students in multiple nations.

Another example of cultural transformation is the Teenangels, a team of young volunteers worldwide who protect their peers online. The organization Cyberangels.org was founded by Parry Aftab, a New York lawyer who trains adult volunteers to monitor chat rooms and teaches young people how they can avoid criminals who prey on children by using email, online chat rooms, and instant messaging. The Teenangels then spread the safety messages at school and through their web site.

Yet another example of cultural transformation through education is the Bilingual Excel Grant at McKinley High School in Buffalo, New York. Teachers here addressed the challenges of linguistic diversity among students as well as the lack of student knowledge and awareness of their larger community and its cultural agencies:

> Students planned a tour of their community using a variety of modes of transportation. Through field trips in which students visited the public libraries, art and historical museums, horticultural gardens, and a butterfly conservatory, they learned to describe and differentiate among the functions of each of these agencies and sites while improving their effective social communication in English. They gained an understanding of the social, historical and cultural diversities within their communities by using various print and technology resources. Students applied learned technological knowledge and skills to design a Web page with the assistance of a consultant. As a result of

working cooperatively with other students throughout this project, they developed cross-cultural skills and an understanding as well as an appreciation of one another. (Kearney, 2000, p. 153)

Although many schools do not have the funding to support student transportation and technology consultants, similar efforts can be replicated by bringing cultural institutions to the school setting through volunteers, guest speakers, and the internet. Whether these connections happen through face-to-face communication or digital communication (or both) is secondary to the larger goal of building bridges between students and the communities in which they live.

Virtual communities muddy the waters of cultural transformation. Virtual worlds are computer-simulated environments that have existed for decades. The most recent trend is Second Life (web-based software) where millions of people are registered as virtual selves or **avatars** that are entirely under the user's control. The sociality occurs as avatars interact with one another and groups form. Similar to simulation software, Second Life is currently the most popular of virtual worlds and it is vast. It consists of houses, stores, offices, and a consumer-driven aspect where businesses offer professional services. From a learning standpoint, virtual worlds allow learners to experiment and learn through doing and observing others. Virtual worlds are social media that may assist the user in increasing a sense of self and even the ability and motivation to socially collaborate. However, they may also be conducive to self-serving or even self-indulgent cooperation rather than collaboration. Cooperation is more passive whereas collaboration requires active effort at building new knowledge. While the user may be able to virtually transform through online social interaction, the hours of online use is based primarily on user convenience. Virtual worlds such as Second Life can undoubtedly detract from local community interaction in the real world. With a myriad of costs and benefits associated with online communities and distance learning, educators should consider the possibilities and pitfalls of the brick-and-mortar classroom of the future. Here are some posits:

Learning in the classroom of the future is neither confined by space nor time. Although more information exists outside of the traditional

Avatar
is a computer icon that represents a person within a virtual community.

classroom than inside, educators confine learning to a square-footage of space. This is, to a certain extent, unavoidable in the business of mass public education. There are tensions that emerge from the necessity of creating classroom compartments that are distinctively labeled *classroom, workshop,* or *laboratory* when these labels should apply to all of the classrooms of the future. Formal schooling may begin at 8:00 a.m. and end at 3:00 p.m., but young people are able to connect with information and communicate with one another 24 hours a day, 7 days a week, from any location via digital technologies. Educators must tap into this resource for accessing and communicating information—not only to increase the efficiency and efficacy of formal schooling but to also cultivate in young people a deeper critical awareness of the information that is so pervasive in their daily lives.

Learning in the classroom of the future involves the use of media technologies that are both portable and transparent. Technically, we can access information anytime and anywhere; iPods, blogs, and PDAs all imply mobility and portability of information. These devices enable collaborative, independent, and differentiated learning—education that is customizable to the unique needs of individual learners. Once teachers and students master the technological skills associated with specific devices (i.e., computers, cell phones, digital cameras), the focus should be on media and information literacies. In this sense, *technology* should not be thought of as a separate subject area, but as a way of seeing and making sense of the world (See Chapter I). Given that some (not all) adults and young people can instantaneously access information in multimedia formats and manipulate, create, and communicate large amounts of data, administrators and leaders are faced with tough questions, such as: "How will our tools empower us to do new things in the class-room?" "What then becomes the function of the (traditional) classroom?" The answers to these and other questions determine how educators design, configure, and equip school buildings and classroom spaces. Considering the convergence of (1) ubiquity of information; (2) portability and mobility afforded by new technologies; and (3) increased technological skills (via NCLB) among young people in the United States, it makes little sense to equip schools with stationary computer laboratories that house bulky equipment that only a portion of students can access during

any given week. The technologies should be transparent to learning, rather than an apparent (and inflexible) distraction. Learning in the classroom of the future should be less about students' technological proficiency and more about their level of media literacy.

Learning in the classroom of the future is less about information access and more about making connections to transform understanding. The continuous exponential increase in the amount of information available in our society places less emphasis on (and need for) memorization of information. The shift in the classroom is, therefore, to make connections across bodies of information, apply principles of understanding, and use new knowledge to solve real problems. Technologies such as videoconferencing support this idea and are assets to the classroom of the future. Although brick-and-mortar classrooms should be equipped for distance learning—to connect to the outside world—the physical space is also a laboratory for building oral communication skills (via face-to-face interaction) and for learning how to graduate from cooperation to *collaboration.*

The classroom of the future is defined not by its technology, rather by its capacity to enable learners to transform knowledge and translate classroom practice into socially responsible action. Despite all the wiring (or wireless access), equipment, and/or "mediation" of a school building, innovative teaching cannot happen without a pedagogical paradigm shift. Teachers can no longer talk at students. Granted, there is a knowledge base and sets of basic skills that students must acquire. However, at some point, students must engage in their own inquiry in order to develop higher-order thinking skills. The result of teaching and learning in the classroom of the future is independent thinking and critically minded problem solving. The challenge lies in the issue of accountability: We hold teachers accountable for teaching students and enacting curriculum. Yet, when the classroom environment (including the technology) is inadequate in support-ing pedagogy, wherein lies the accountability? Too often we blame the teachers for their neophyte approach to technology; we blame even the machines themselves. However, a more fruitful approach is to develop more authentic school- and community-wide structures that promote instructional accountability, authority, and respect at all levels. As educators we must face any and all residual fears about the digital world—where files corrupt, computers crash, and windows collapse. Although there may be

room for skeptical rejection of these network technologies, they are nevertheless powerful environments in which to educate young people about choice and accountability.

While some young people may be more technologically proficient than adults, many are not. For example, college students may be wired, but they lack the critical thinking skills and the moral framework in which to navigate their educational experiences and even personal lives with wisdom and vision. A major concern among college professors is the lack of information, communications, and technological (ICT) literacy among incoming freshman. Certainly the internet has increased the level of user access to information and user anonymity, creating a fertile environment for cheating and plagiarism. This, in turn, creates additional avenues and responsibilities for teachers and administrators to detect and stop student plagiarism. It is difficult to discern to what extent plagiarism is intentional and to what extent it is done in ignorance.

Similarly, many teachers are unsure about what material they themselves can use in the classroom without permission. It is erroneous to think that anything can be used in the classroom under the banner of **Fair Use**. In an effort to enliven class lecture and discussion, many teachers download images, video, audio, and web sites to incorporate into their curriculum, yet without fully understanding copyright and Fair Use guidelines. For example, under Fair Use a teacher can use copyright-protected images in a PowerPoint presentation to instruct his/her class but cannot upload that presentation to the World Wide Web without permission from the copyright holder(s). While teachers may desire to compile a collection (on one VHS tape or a single DVD) of video clips from major Hollywood films, it is not a provision of the Fair Use guidelines and, therefore, violates copyright law. *Technology & Learning* magazine (http://www.techlearning.com) provides educators with a chart that maps the fair uses and copyright restrictions of each medium (e.g., print, photographs, video, music, software, TV broadcasts), including how much content can be used and under what conditions. Such teacher education in the legalities and ethics of intellectual property and copyright law is essential, given that students themselves need to understand the constraints as well as possibilities of sharing information in a knowledge society. It is crucial than educators lead through

Fair Use

is part of the U.S. copyright law that allows limited use of copyrighted material without obtaining written permission, purchasing the work, or paying the author a royalty.

example. Not only must intellectual property rights and laws surrounding copyright and fair use be magnified at instructional levels, but district policies, procedures, and technological infrastructure must also reflect an understanding of adherence to such guidelines. Along a similar vein, information literacy—traditionally the curricular responsibility of the librarian, now known as the library media specialist—must converge with formal classroom curriculum. In other words, asking critical questions relative to content, authority, credibility, and usefulness of information must proliferate through all subject areas and all classroom curricula—and occur not only in the library or computer lab. In other words, media, technology, and information literacies must converge and serve as a wide lens through which to view curriculum, instruction, and schooling in general.

Our biggest educational challenge is, therefore, pedagogical and not solely technological. Rather than continuously asking, "How can this technology support my curriculum?" we need to reframe the conversation about technology by asking, "How can teachers prepare students to be critical consumers and users of information?" "How can teacher education programs better prepare teachers and administrators to be critical consumers and users of information?" This chapter raises the question "How can we move beyond technology as content management into more advanced uses of technology that culturally transforms the world in positive and meaningful ways?" Indeed, cultural transformation requires the belief that the skillful use of digital media and technology can actually promote social justice, for which technological proficiency is prerequisite. Yet technological proficiency is not enough. Diverse populations that comprise the educational system in the United States must also subscribe to a responsible citizenship perspective of media, technology, culture, and education. The turnkey from content management to cultural transformation is a deeper understanding of human communication coupled with technological proficiency. Ultimately, if we expand our understanding of the classroom to be a discursive community where students together generate and transform information for social change, then *technology* denotes something much more meaningful and valuable than a set of tools or information delivery systems.

Glossary

Web 2.0—refers to the second generation of the World Wide Web and is characterized by applications and data residing on the web.

Rich media—refers to advanced technology that allows for media interactivity (combining text, audio, and video) as well as interactive experiences on the part of the user.

Pedagogy—the art and science of teaching. The term also refers to strategies or styles of teaching.

Hierarchy of needs—is a psychological theory set forth by Abraham Maslow in 1943. It is usually depicted as a pyramid consisting of five levels: Physiological, safety, love/belonging, esteem, and self-actualization. The first four levels are characterized as physiological and the top level is associated with psychological needs.

Open source—is a set of principles and practices on how to write software, the source code for which is openly available.

Discussion boards—are internet communities for holding discussions and posting user-generated content.

Asynchronous mode—refers to communication that is not existing or happening at the same time.

Global Positioning System (GPS)—is a global navigation satellite system that enables a GPS receiver to determine its location, speed, direction, and time.

YouTube—is a video-sharing web site created in 2005 where users can upload, view, and share video clips. In July 2006, 100 million videos were being watched everyday.

TeacherTube—is an online community for uploading, viewing, and sharing instructional videos related to student learning and teacher professional development.

SchoolTube—is a media-sharing website for teachers and students in K-12 schools. The site is moderated and requires that all student created content follow local school guidelines and be approved by registered teachers before it is made available on the Web.

Social networking sites—are online communities of people who share interests and activities. They provide various ways for users to interact, such as messaging, email, video, file sharing, blogging, and discussion groups.

iPodagogy—is the study of teaching methods using iPods or other handheld audio and/or video devices.

Liberatory pedagogy—is the practice of education for liberation or critical pedagogy. It incorporates a struggle for meaning as well as a struggle for freedom and justice.

Cybercitizen—is a person who is actively involved in online communities and uses the internet to engage in activities that are socially and/or politically responsible.

Avatar—is a computer icon that represents a person within a virtual community.

Fair Use—is part of the U.S. copyright law that allows limited use of copyrighted material without obtaining written permission, purchasing the work, or paying the author a royalty.

CHAPTER FOUR

Technology Leadership

Integrating curriculum and technology within the complex and often chaotic environment of schooling is a bold endeavor even for the most seasoned and tech-savvy teacher. For school systems with existing imbalances such as high dropout rate, low parental involvement, and disciplinary problems, integrating technology and curriculum is likely to be disregarded as an extracurricular burden rather than as a means of counteracting such systemic imbalances. The bureaucratic pressure to achieve technological literacy at the same time burdens school leaders with additional budget constraints, technological obsolescence, security and access challenges, and increased accountability through formalized assessments. As of 2007, the No Child Left Behind law requires all eighth graders to be tested for technological literacy. States delegate such testing to local districts, which in turn delegate the responsibility to the computer or business teacher. Amid these challenges and changes, one thing is clear: The role of the classroom teacher remains of paramount importance. At the same time, the need for teacher professional development is longstanding and unmet in the area of instructional technology. The frontier efforts of teacher-pioneers who forge

new technological ground on their own time with little, if any, compensation do not constitute a sustainable model. School leaders must instead learn to navigate complex administrative challenges while cultivating and supporting **technology leadership** among teachers.

There is a key distinction to be made between the idea of technology leadership and the idea of merely administering technology. The difference lies in the ability of educators to anchor their teaching practices with a larger vision or purpose. Technology leadership requires the development of strategies that empower individuals to enact a common vision. Kotter (1999) observes that "leadership works through people and culture. It's soft and hot. Administration works through hierarchy and systems. It's harder and cooler" (p. 10). Administration of technology involves planning, budgeting, organizing, staffing, and problem solving. If effective technology leadership does not accompany effective technology administration, the results are mismatched priorities and needs.

An Ecological Approach

Technology leadership implies a **systemic view** of technology, particularly as to the communication environments that surround the uses of technology in schools. Different strands of ecology woven together serve as a useful basis for rethinking technology in schools. **Media ecology** is a field of study concerned with the impact of technologies on other environments, such as family, government, business, and education. Just as in natural ecology the air, land, and water are interconnected and impact one another, so are social, political, economic, media, and education institutions interdependent. Media ecologists are also interested in how technology has been adopted, institutionalized, and used and by whom. They make the connections between technology and broader social and political issues, as well as how power is gained and maintained through different forms of communication.

Not all technologies are equal in their force since their influences are contingent upon the complexity of their existing environments. Questions school leaders might ask include: How has the evolution of a particular communications technology, such as the internet, changed teaching, learning, and schooling? Are there unintended consequences of using social networking

---

Technology leadership
is the development of technological infrastructures and pedagogical strategies that empower educators to enact a common curricular vision.

Systemic view
of technology looks at educational systems and environments, rather than specific technologies.

Media ecology
is a field of study concerned with the impact of technologies on environments such as family, government, business, and education.

in education? If so, how are these consequences currently manifested? Collateral risks of social networking may include child predators and cyberbullying. Are these potential consequences formally addressed in an Acceptable Use Policy? The impact of social networking technologies on schooling can be understood only through its relationship to broader political, social, economic, educational, and familial environments. In other words, it is never strictly about the relationship between user and the machine.

The goal is to help humans become both conscious and conscientious of communication environments and their elements. In this light, technology leaders must examine the components of a school environment or culture to fully understand the potential influence of a particular technology. They must also closely examine the relationship between leadership, administration, student needs, curriculum, teaching, assessment, professional development, organizational communication, and resource allocation. Technology is merely one element within an interdependent system of families, communities, businesses, religious institutions, and government. Nardi and O'Day (1999) provide a useful framework of an **information ecology** where the focus is on human activities that are served keeping the technologies as one component of a larger system. An ecological approach to the classroom considers how educational and instructional technologies are defined: what resources are selected to mediate instruction, the physical setting in which technologies are used and/or taught (e.g., classroom vs. laboratory), by whom it is taught, as well as the student environment. Principals might facilitate discussions with teachers about how and why learning occurs through the mediation of information through technologies and how it shapes *what* students learn (and do not learn).

There are multiple levels of structure, communication, and vision that must be established in schools to cultivate technology leadership among administrators and teachers. Just as schools are a component of a larger community system, so are teachers a component of the larger school organization. With National Educational Technology Standards (NETS) and the push for technological literacy, there is tremendous pressure on teachers to use new(er) technologies to support their curricula. Yet, schools have played almost no role in helping teachers develop the critical thinking skills necessary to use new media and technologies

Information ecology
is a system of people, practices, values, and technologies in a particular local environment.

well. Sadly, professional development is often thought of as an afternoon or an all-day training session on how to use a computer or a piece of software. In contrast, an ecological framework for technology leadership situates the educator as an empowered orchestra leader who uses a variety of resources to create a classroom environment that supports a shared vision for teaching and learning.

Rethinking Professional Development

As teachers, how do we come to know that chalkboards, whiteboards, film, TV, computers, and the internet are all tools to help us teach and to help students learn? Perhaps it is through our own schooling experiences as students? Or maybe through a course or two within our teacher preparation program? For the majority of teachers, it is neither. Recent reports assert that teacher education programs do not adequately prepare preservice teachers to integrate technology into their teaching (Bell 2001, Levine 2006). The popular mechanism of sending teachers to workshops or providing "just-in-time" professional development may help establish a core base of technical skills and knowledge. However, teachers need time to reflect on and contemplate the ways in which specific technologies shape curriculum for better or worse. This requires sustained interaction with a variety of technologies (and their associated media texts) and time to collectively share one's understandings and professional insights with colleagues. It follows that in-service teacher education programs should provide more than just technical instruction in the latest digital technologies.

At the same time, professional development is a transformative process that begins with basic experimentation and grows as teachers gain experience using technology to enact curriculum. Professional development must enable and support teacher inquiry (into subject matter, student learning, and teaching practice), so that teachers can adapt their practices in ways appropriate to the demands of the subject matter and their students' learning. Research further indicates that educational professionals need time, resources, and collegial support to experiment with and implement new ideas to effect changes in the classroom. Teachers' belief in the value of a technology increases as they gain exposure to it and as students use it directly.

Teachers require not only technical training but also training in how specific technologies can be integrated into ongoing curricular activities. More than just learning the tools, thoughtful technology integration implies a process of curriculum design, implementation, assessment, and redesign. Unfortunately, this type of professional development is often seen as a luxury that school budgets cannot afford. Considering all the administrative tasks that teachers are responsible for, it is not surprising that tackling the complex and sometimes painful task of using technology to support (and not detract from) classroom teaching is a low priority. Depending upon the culture of the school, principals might support ongoing professional development through program-scheduled class visitation, per-session compensation for after-school planning sessions, and release from administrative duty.

The ideal is to establish a network of teachers that will continue to expand as they share with one another their successes and failures with using technology in the classroom. According to Michael Fullan (2007), development of **professional learning communities** (PLCs) is critical to sustaining and generating teacher change. Such communities provide a climate for engaging in inquiry, sharing knowledge of student thinking, sharing norms for what counts as effective instruction and student achievement, and building social supports for managing the uncertainty and ever-evolving nature of communications technology. Although strategies for building structures to sustain long-term teacher professional development vary, research shows that they all involve substantial restructuring of schooling to enhance collaboration between teachers and administrators. Such restructuring assists teachers in developing the resources necessary to conduct practical inquiry and in sharing the results with a larger community. Fullan also asserts that any type of sustained educational change requires, in addition to restructuring schools, a "reculturing" of the school environment. Educators should be mindful of the three dimensions of teacher development: personal, professional, and pedagogical.

Professional learning community

describes a professional development approach where a collegial group of educators become united through a common purpose. They work and learn collaboratively and participate in collective decision making for the sake of educational renewal.

Three Stages of Technology Professional Development

Professional development is best understood as a carefully planned series and/or a combination of experiences through

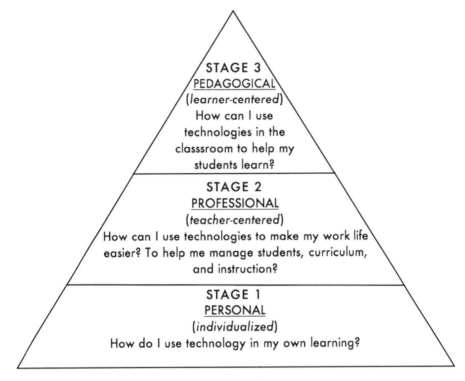

Figure 4 Stages of Technology Professional Development

which teachers come to an understanding of how specific technologies influence their personal, professional, and pedagogical lives. Such development requires educators to move through three stages of conceptualizing technology (see Figure 4).

On a personal level, educators may use technologies such as cell phones, email, and digital cameras. They then have experiences on which to reflect on the impact of technologies on their own communication and ways of living. In this initial stage, educators may have definite opinions about technologies in their own lives (i.e., "I can't live without my cell phone") but may have relatively unexamined or even contradictory opinions on the same technologies in school (i.e., "students try to cheat on exams with their cell phones, so they must power them off in class").

The professional stage may encompass on-the-job training in using computerized grading systems or computer-based testing as well as in sending email to communicate with principals and colleagues. The uses of technology at this level are primarily administrative and are not directly linked to student learning.

As teachers become more web savvy and better skilled to identify "teacher help" web sites, they learn that material already exists from which to draw when preparing their lessons. Teachers might use call phones to communicate with one another on campus, to check their email, and to receive emergency notifications while on the job.

The third stage shifts the focus from the teacher's personal and professional concerns to student-centered needs and identifiable curricular outcomes. Ideally, the uses of technology at this level should directly support curriculum and be integrated within the curriculum and instruction environments. At this stage, a teacher has both personal and professional experience with a particular technology and can effectively manage student uses of the technology. A teacher might require her students to use their cell phone to text message one another as part of a collaborative writing assignment. The teacher during a field trip might ask students to use their cell phones to take photos that they can later incorporate into a multimedia project. The possibilities are limitless. Yet, ascension to these more complex pedagogical uses of technology requires much planning and coordination.

The Importance of Technology Planning

Given that policy and standards frame technology primarily as a skills-based curriculum destination (rather than a method of thinking and learning about the world), it is not surprising that most technology planning consists of little more than an inventory of equipment. For the purposes of this book, a technology plan identifies systemic elements that support a specific curriculum goal. A technology plan is, therefore, a tangible road map to student achievement of specific subject area standards and not just standards in the area of technological literacy.

Given that school environments are complex and ever changing, a technology plan should be thought of as a living document that is continuously evolving and adapting to serve the felt needs within a particular school environment—whether it be born and implemented at the district, school, department, or classroom levels. Technology leaders must make it a priority to discover the felt needs within a school culture through constant communication with and among administrators, teachers, and students. In this sense, technology planning is a communal and

dialogic process that catalyzes and redefines curriculum to reflect the collective needs of students and teachers. It is, therefore, essential that technology leaders carve out opportunities for teachers and administrators to collectively brainstorm and vocalize concerns, and to articulate needs and wants relative to curriculum planning and technology acquisition.

Such dialogue requires critical thinking about the dominant assumptions and practices of students, teachers, administrators, and the larger system of schooling. It is important that these conversations are cultivated through inquiry, rather than criticism or cynicism, and fueled by a genuine motivation to more deeply understand curriculum and teaching.

Technology planning and implementation require a clearly outlined structure for communication. A planning committee ideally consists of an eclectic group of participants who are collectively knowledgeable about the school culture and can collegially work together to identify available media and technology resources, standards and assessments, organizational communication structures, means of ongoing support, professional development needs, and the leadership required to use technology to transform teaching and learning.

The principal is an essential part of this dialogue because (s)he can often answer basic essential questions related to funding, school planning, and intradepartmental issues that can move the planning process along more rapidly. It is important to consider what departments, interests, and/or needs are to be represented by a technology planning committee. What are the communication structures between and among instruction, administration, departments, technicians, other schools, and district leaders? Just as the principal needs to shape the planning process, the planning committee needs to shape the forms of leadership and give it the support it needs, through constant communication with the principal.

Within the school culture, the responsibility for curriculum and technology integration is often misdirected towards a technology coordinator, who most likely is a technician or administrator rather than a teacher. Given the numerous responsibilities of principals, technology coordinators, teachers, and administrators, the internal structure of shared leadership depends upon the school climate. Does the principal govern like a CEO of a corporation? President? Orchestra leader? Coach? As with most committees, the principal must ensure that individual members of the technology planning committee are valued to give weight to the communal and collaborative process. Although the principal may not provide much input or expertise in the area of technology, the contribution may come as ongoing support in the form of release time, equipment, or professional development.

It is common for technology planning to stall in the technical talk, particularly when the topic involves the desire for newer and faster machines or the logistics surrounding issues of security and access. After all, what teacher is not intrigued to some degree by a cart of new personal digital assistants (PDAs) or the academic possibilities of using cell phones in coursework? Although discussions about tangible equipment may be exciting for some educators, in reality those technical conversations lend minimal, if any, support to innovation and change when it comes to curriculum and teaching. Educational purpose must foreshadow the uses of technology. Ideally, curriculum (as collectively defined) should drive the acquisition, configuration, distribution, and maintenance of instructional technologies in schools. Technology planning as a vehicle for curriculum innovation and more democratic practice requires educators to defer, if only momentarily, technical issues to deliberate what students should know and how they best learn particular content areas.

In sum, a technology plan is site-based, collectively created, and curriculum-driven and spans a designated period of time. At its most basic and local level, technology planning requires goal setting, marshaling physical and human resources, and establishing structures for implementation and ongoing support.

Initiating the Planning Process

The daily life of a teacher is, to a certain extent, clouded by federal mandates, standards, and policies. Teachers face an uphill battle as they are required through No Child Left Behind to ensure that all students achieve technological literacy by the end of eighth grade. Such evidence is collected through standardized tests that are yet to be fully developed by the teachers themselves. Technology is a topic that evokes a variety of emotional responses among teachers. It is, therefore, imperative that administrators enact leadership in this area in recognizing, supporting, and compensating

teachers in the thoughtful planning, implementing, and enacting of curriculum and technology integration. It is, therefore, essential to convene a technology planning committee of teachers, administrators, and school leaders who are committed to (and compensated for) meeting regularly during the course of the school year.

The process of successful technology planning begins with an autobiographical exercise that compels educators to reflect upon and articulate their own personal, professional, and pedagogical relationships to technology, to understand their own biases towards the tools themselves. Technology leaders can start the conversation by posing the question, "What three communications technologies have influenced you the most on a personal level?" Narrowing their selection to only three compels educators to cull responses that reflect their daily technology habits and dispositions or to dig deeper into those media technologies that have strongly impacted them earlier on in their lives. The most common response is the ubiquitous television. Many educators include cell phones (which have recently achieved ubiquitous status) and computers and internet (which are usually lumped together as one technology). Interestingly, teachers rarely list books or other print media in their top three, despite the reality that schooling is still predominantly print-based and focused on print literacy.

This autobiographical exercise is illuminating, both for individual teachers and the collective group, as it reflects perceptions of technology's impact on our personal and professional identities. A teacher may think (s)he cannot live without a cell phone (and thus it is number one on her list) when books and TV have actually influenced her more deeply as a learner. These technology autobiographies are collectively shared and the group discussion centers on the hidden assumptions and hierarchies they construct about the role of technology in their personal and professional lives. This autobiographical exercise is also an opportunity to acknowledge different perceptions of technology and various perspectives on its impact. One educator may write "pen and paper," much to the surprise of his/her colleagues who had not considered such material as "technology." The conversation can then evolve into a discussion about which technologies are accessible within schools and classrooms on a regular basis.

Interestingly, textbooks and overhead projectors may be the most commonly accessible instructional technologies in the school classroom and, at the same time, the least influential in the personal and professional lives of teachers. The disconnection between school and personal technology use is a significant one that should be discussed. This technology autobiography exercise provides a springboard for novice and veteran teachers alike to begin to articulate their philosophy of teaching as it pertains to the curriculum and how that curriculum is communicated and constructed. It is foundational to the curriculum and technology integration process.

Technology leaders can facilitate the discussion to a pedagogical level by posing the question: "What are the three communications technologies that you think have influenced your students the most?" Depending upon the extent to which they are connected to young people and know their lives outside of school, teachers might think their students perceive cell phones (text-messaging) as the most influential communications technology. Other responses might include mp3 players and video games. The idea in this phase of the autobiographical exercise is to acknowledge the differences and locate the similarities between the teachers' lists and the students' lists. The commonality usually extends as far as the hardware (computer and internet, cell phone) rather than applications or uses. In other words, both groups may regularly use the internet, but a young person might be gaming while the teacher is researching information. Similarly, the teacher may use a cell phone on a regular basis, but not in the same way as her students. Ideally, a teacher would ask the students themselves to list their three most influential communications technologies for a deeper understanding of their communication (and ultimately learning) styles and to locate the (dis)connections between students' technology use outside the classroom as compared to within the four walls of the classroom. This stage of inquiry should begin to connect for teachers their philosophy of and expectations for technology with their own practical knowledge of students and the instructional resources that exist.

If we compare our autobiographies to those of our students, do we see any commonalities? How might we establish a technological community to which every student and teacher has intellectual and physical access? There lies a disjunction between

what teachers expect from the technologies of education and what they believe teaching to be. This disjunction often occurs as a result of misconceptions about technology—that it will solve all problems—or a lack of awareness among teachers about best pedagogical practices.

How often are teachers asked to articulate their teaching philosophy as it relates to technology? Do we not hold teachers accountable for instructing students and facilitating curriculum? When the technological environments are ineffective in supporting teachers' felt needs, wherein lies the accountability? The solution lies not in attributing blame but rather in developing better (more authentic) school- and community-wide structures that promote instructional and technological accountability. An inquiry-based approach to technology planning addresses these philosophical, practical, and pedagogical dimensions (see Table I).

Establishing a Common Vision

A positive relationship exists between teachers who establish educational goals and objectives and the ways in which they are able to integrate technology into their classroom teaching. In this way, a technology plan is more than a useful map for curriculum and instruction. Of equal importance are the active communal process of planning as well as the dialogic accomplishment of a unified vision and a set of curriculum goals that technology can support. It is no small task to achieve unity of purpose among educators while at the same time privileging diversity of curricula and teaching styles. However, this dialogic process is essential to cultivating a sense of empowerment rather than oppression among teachers. A technology leader strives for a collective commitment to a common educational goal at which all resources converge.

A successful technology plan flows from an articulated educational vision. Some school administrators wrap their vision in language that is highly abstract and void of local meaning, as seen, for instance, in a school or district mission statement (i.e., creating lifelong learners). In arriving at a vision statement, technology leaders and a planning committee together mine commonalities across district and school statements, and across local and national educational trends, to identify and prioritize areas for improvement at a local level. The challenge is to operationally define the educational vision through articulated goal(s).

Table I Three Domains of Inquiry About Technology in Schools

PHILOSOPHICAL *Establishing a Common Vision* <u>Educational Goal(s)</u>	• What is your leadership style as school leader? • What are the core content curriculum standards? • What are the vision and/or mission of the school district and/or the larger community? • What goal or theme is your school or department pursuing at this time? • What do you want students to know or be able to do?
PRACTICAL *Taking Inventory* <u>Instructional Resources</u>	• What media/technologies do students use in their lives beyond the classroom? • What media/technologies exist onsite? • What do the bodies of technology standards for teachers and students require? • What media/technologies are teachers already familiar with? Who are the technology leaders? • Are there any media/technologies that may detract from curricular goals?
PEDAGOGICAL *Implementation* <u>Teaching Strategies</u>	• What is the relationship between teaching and the larger school culture? • How do students learn best? • What are the "best practices" or teaching strategies that teachers currently use? How can they be expanded? • How can the media literacy cycle of access, analyze, evaluate, produce, and communicate be integrated into the teaching repertoire across the faculty?

Sources for educational goals can be state and national curriculum standards, school and district mission statements, an existing comprehension education plan, set of local curriculum priorities, a school's annual theme, or even government sanctions imposed upon a school "in need of improvement." Examples of an operationally defined vision might include increasing math scores, enhancing reading skills, cultivating multicultural awareness, or deepening understanding of world history. For technology planning, the designated goal should be broad enough to support cross-disciplinary collaboration among teachers, yet focused enough to directly support specific strands of curriculum standards.

Occasionally, teachers entangle themselves in the multiple strands of curriculum standards: state core content curriculum standards, national standards within subject areas, National Educational Technology Standards (for teachers and students). Technology leaders can help teachers to untangle the standards through the technology planning process by visually mapping curriculum so that standards are at the forefront of their teaching, and to ensure that the technologies serve a supporting role. Neither technological literacy nor acquisition of specific equipment is part of the educational goal at this point, as these are part of the methods of achieving the goal and not the actual curriculum goal. Although assessment is rarely thought of as part of the planning process, it is essential to establish benchmarks early on, particularly in the current climate of high-stakes testing.

Identifying Resources

Once a technology planning committee decides on a vision and accordingly its goals, they can then devote direct and sustained attention toward the technologies themselves. Here technology leaders and teachers can indulge in their fascination with particular tools and devices. The end point of this phase is the creation of a comprehensive inventory of media and technology that is actually accessible at a given school site or district. Information about available technologies can often be found in an existing school or district technology inventory or even in a library media curriculum. Another strategy is to ask the school secretary, who is often knowledgeable about what is available and where it is kept.

The purpose of taking a comprehensive inventory is greater than counting computers and software. Equally valuable are instructional technologies that include manipulatives, books, TVs, VCRs, overhead projectors, microphones, cameras, and audio recorders—in addition to personal digital assistants, electronic whiteboards, and tablet PCs. Consulting a district or school technology plan or even library plan (if such documents exist) is a viable way to discover what equipment resides at the site and to become familiar with the school's history. Creating a technology inventory allows teachers to: (1) Locate technologies that are currently accessible at their school site and thus are real options for their teaching; (2) Identify technology professional development needs; and (3) Create a tangible document that will allow teachers to restrain technology-dominant conversations to focus on core curriculum content development.

When the inventory is as comprehensive as possible, an important next step is to organize the inventory into the following categories, based on function: Research (e.g., search engines, databases, periodicals); presentation tools (e.g., charts, maps, PowerPoint), data gathering (e.g., audio/video recorders, PDAs with probes); simulation (e.g., mock trial, SimCity software, virtual frog dissection web site, Second Life), authoring (e.g., crayons, markers, drafting supplies, multimedia authoring software such as Microsoft Office, Flash, Dreamweaver, and web-based applications), and communication (e.g., public address system, email, text-messaging, cell phones, TV production, podcasting software). Marshaling resources involves taking a snapshot of the whole school system and of places where specific (dis)connections among resources might occur. Conversations include technical issues such as access, space, and programming, as well as immediate concerns about student test scores, professional development, classroom management, and curriculum.

At this stage professional development needs and interests should be acknowledged and discussed, particularly if there is a felt need among teachers for initial exposure to technologies that currently exist on site. Preliminary hands-on experimentation with existing technology allows teachers the frame of reference necessary to ponder their functions and how they shape curriculum as well as pedagogy. Taking inventory also makes more explicit the need for technical skills even at the most basic level. During this

initial phase, teachers may voice existing needs for professional development. These may or may not be technologically related. Although technology should not be a goal in and of itself, it is important to recognize that educators need much time to experiment and "play" with the tools—achieve a minimum level of proficiency—before conceptualizing their administrative and/or pedagogical potential.

Creating a running inventory of all resources available widens the pedagogical possibilities and the inroads to achieving curriculum standards. Decentralizing information about (and eventually access to) these technologies is a powerful step in democratizing technology in schools. An additional step is to review the inventory and ask, "Which of these technologies do my students use on a regular basis?" It is worthwhile for technology leaders to survey students about the technologies they access and use on a regular basis outside of school. Students may use cell phones, video games, and instant messaging outside the classroom and yet encounter foreign technological texts (such as books) in the classroom. It is important for technology leaders to recognize the digital divide that exists between the school technology inventory and the technologies young people have access to outside of school.

The academic uses of technologies to support instruction are frequently mired in the administration of them. This poses a huge stumbling block, particularly to teachers new to computers, for example. Issues of access and control are huge stumbling blocks to instruction (e.g., appropriate software, computer lab entry, security). It is understandable that the administrative conversations must address real issues of security and maintenance of resources. At the same time, however, these policies must support the instructional needs of teachers. This is difficult to do when teachers have not engaged in conversations about their curriculum and what they need in terms of technological support. Teachers should be encouraged to identify the type of instructional environments and then work with administrators to establish technological frameworks to support those environments.

Implementing a Technology Plan

Neither the quantity nor the quality of technological resources available dictates the extent to which technology is or

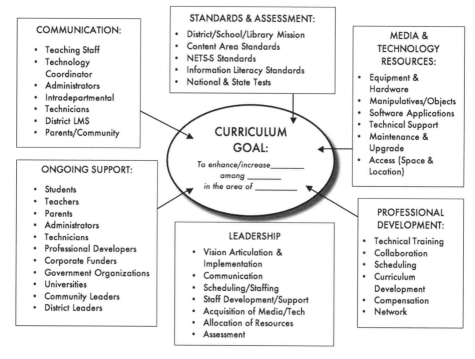

Figure 5 Systemic Technology Planning

can be used to support curriculum and collaboration. Rather, the uses of technology are contingent upon a balanced system that includes elements of leadership, professional development, ongoing support, and communication (see Figure 5).

Once an educational goal and support structures are identified, the next step is the creation of support structures for implementing and achieving the educational goal. This requires continuous support, the responsibility for which ultimately falls on the principal. As the overseer of programs, personnel, and curriculum, the principal is at the helm to navigate all three phases of the technology planning process. Ironically, the ever-increasing demands placed upon principals make it nearly impossible to sustain educational change. It is the establishment of internal and external structures of shared leadership that allows principals to be wise stewards over technology in schools. While some principals may justify their lack of involvement in technology as leadership from below, the reality is that a technology plan cannot be realized without the principal as steward of the processes of initiation, identification of resources, and implementation.

The principal, in a stance external to the school culture, exercises technology leadership by cultivating partnerships with families, community members, private and public business leaders, alumni, local college students, and local and district leaders. Technology can directly support these efforts through social networking technologies that widen the school community: a school web site that incorporates blogging and podcasting to keep parents informed and to facilitate communication and opportunities for contributing to the educational goal of the technology plan. One urban high school principal in Detroit, inspired by the technological savvy of her college-age children, chose to acquire computers and internet access specifically for increasing parental involvement in schools within the district. The principal creatively assembled Title I funding and business partnerships to build electronic networks between district schools and neighborhood housing developments. This orchestration of funding included monies for a technology coordinator and two computer labs, both in schools and within housing developments. The principal supported community professional development in which parents, teachers, and families collaborated on web pages for their classrooms and schools. The web pages announced school activities and hosted discussion threads for interaction among teachers, students, and parents. What is particularly powerful about this systemic approach to technology is its insight into the importance of family and community support in increasing student achievement. Particularly powerful is reframing professional development as a communal activity that involves students, families, teachers, and members of the community. The lesson here is that principals and local administrators must not only be a part of the process but also lead, implement, sustain, and support it along the way.

Glossary

Technology leadership—is the development of technological infrastructures and pedagogical strategies that empower educators to enact a common curricular vision.

Systemic view—of technology looks at educational systems and environments, rather than specific technologies.

Media ecology—is a field of study concerned with the impact of technologies on environments such as family, government, business, and education.

Information ecology—is a system of people, practices, values, and technologies in a particular local environment.

Professional learning community—describes a professional development approach where a collegial group of educators become united through a common purpose. They work and learn collaboratively and participate in collective decision making for the sake of educational renewal.

CHAPTER FIVE

Curriculum and Technology Integration

Integration

is the combining and coordinating of separate parts or elements into a unified whole. It requires a much more complex orchestration of activities than merely using high-tech devices in schooling.

Technology integration is often associated with the haphazard uses of new technologies, often separate and disconnected from curriculum. Yet the term **integration** actually denotes the combining and coordinating of separate parts or elements into a unified whole. It requires a much more complex orchestration of activities than merely using high-tech devices in schooling. A precursor to curriculum and technology integration is achieving the widest possible repertoire of instructional media technologies available. This involves knowing how to select the most appropriate technologies, based on (1) identifiable curriculum goal(s) for students; and (2) the ability of the technology to support pedagogical practice that will achieve the curriculum goal(s). In short, the theory and practice of technology integration need to be inextricably connected to the processes and products of curriculum development. This chapter looks at technology planning from a micro-perspective to explore the ways in which teachers can critically and creatively integrate: (1) curriculum goals; (2) pedagogical strategies; and (3) technology resources. This process of aligning goals, strategies, and technologies is both discursive and reflective.

Integration as Reflective Practice

In *The Reflective Practitioner*, Donald Schön (1983) describes how professionals think or improvise in action. He argues for an "epistemology of practice" based on the idea of reflection-in-action. That is, the professional can enlarge or clarify theory by reframing problems encountered through trial and error. This values intuition, as teachers often know more than they can articulate. But Schön reasons that if a teacher can articulate a problem or viewpoint within a context and ask new questions of it, then (s)he comes to a new understanding of the problem and can apply knowledge in more meaningful ways. Schön's work corresponds with the **constructivist** approach to teaching and learning: It is through situational contexts that teachers and students acquire new understandings as they compare new and unfamiliar ideas with previously established ones. This is a useful theory to apply to teacher professional development in the area of technology.

Constructivism is a theory of learning based on the idea that humans actively construct their own knowledge based on their own perceptions and understandings.

A reflective approach requires a departure from the traditional model of teacher as holder of knowledge and the student as knowledge recipient. Instead, professional development is a teaching act between teacher (as learner) and technology leader (as co-learner). Technology leaders should not necessarily provide teachers with a conceptual framework first; rather, a more successful approach guides teachers through an unencumbered exploration of a new domain (i.e., new curriculum or new technology—but not both at the same time) and then through the construction of concepts and skills related to the new domain. This learning model allows the teacher to use new technologies to support a felt need in the classroom, rather than fall into the common trap of using curriculum to serve the use of technology. More often than not, the bells and whistles of the internet, a new piece of software program, or an interactive whiteboard distract both teachers and students from the actual curricular purpose and perpetuate the myth of technological omnipotence in education. The primary role of the professional developer is to ground all discussions of technology within a teacher's own curriculum goals.

Generating a curricular purpose for using technology requires much dialogue and a significant investment in time. Applying

Schön's model of reflective practice, the professional developer engages the teacher in conversation with the curriculum, reframes the problem or challenge, and then moves the dialogue through a pattern of possibilities and/or implications. This reflection in action results in newly developed ideas or solutions. The key for the professional developer is to maintain a rhythm between involvement and detachment—allowing the teacher to generate new possibilities rather than the professional developer prescribing technological solutions. The role of the professional developer is, therefore, limited to framing the issues and defining the necessary skills to enact them, similar to connecting theory with practice. On the surface, the process may appear rather academic; however, the starting point of professional development should be the teacher's felt need.

The following excerpts illustrate a conversation between Ms. Jones, a fifth-grade science teacher in an urban public elementary school, and a professional developer. The consultation was arranged after the principal urged all the lower-grade teachers to use the newly acquired computer hardware and multimedia software in their classrooms:

> MJ: We really need to get high-speed internet so that we can get faster internet access. Also, I'm trying to convince our technology coordinator to get a system upgrade this year.
>
> PD: Okay. Let's think through a curriculum project that uses the equipment that you already have to support your current goals and objectives. However, I'd be happy to talk with you at a later time about how your school might go wireless and let you know how some other schools have set up their system.
>
> MJ: Oh, that would be great.

Whether it is to vent out harbored frustrations or to seek technical expertise, teachers, like most people, get distracted by the technology gadgets at the expense of the curriculum it allegedly supports. The exchange above shows how the professional developer acknowledges the teacher's concerns as legitimate, yet out of place in the context of this particular meeting. In a firm, yet respectful, tone the professional developer diverts the conversation from practical concerns towards more philosophical and

pedagogical courses of action:

> PD: So, what lessons are you going to be working on during the next few weeks?
>
> MJ: The students have to learn the periodic table of elements. I want them to learn each element and memorize the symbol for it and its location on the table.
>
> PD: How do you usually teach them the periodic table?
>
> MJ: I just give them a copy of the table and have them fill it in. I also give them weekly quizzes. But it's all so uninteresting to them.
>
> PD: So, you're saying you wan to spice the lesson up?
>
> MJ: Yes. And I want them to be able to really think about the elements and how they are combined.
>
> PD: Have your students in the past showed interested in competitive games? Do they enjoy presentations?
>
> MJ: Yes, but they usually don't help students think about the elements. They tend to get caught up in the game and usually get too rambunctious.
>
> PD: What about working in groups?
>
> MJ: Actually, they work pretty well together, if I assign groups.

The professional developer continues to shape the conversation to elicit from the teacher her teaching style and preference by asking questions about the teacher design that is currently in place, or what the teacher envisions for future lessons. Although challenging, it is possible to engage in a discussion about curriculum and technology integration in the absence of the technology. The key is to consistently anchor dialogue in the teacher's own felt pedagogical need. Few teachers will learn multimedia-authoring software, for example, just for the sake of acquiring the technical skills. However, once they understand what the software allows them to do personally and even profession-ally, teachers are one step closer to findings ways to enhance their pedagogy. However, the pedagogical step is the most difficult and complicated to reach. The key is to identify what the teacher wants to teach and to then discover what strategies will support it. Only then can the technology enter the conversation.

Rather than imposing a prefabricated curricular design ("what has worked for other teachers"), the professional developer

gathers information about the teaching context by asking questions and then gently moving the teacher to generate possible project ideas:

> PD: So, you want the students to learn or memorize each element and its place on the table. Is there some sort of project you could assign them that would use the periodic table in a unique way? That would require them to really know the elements?
>
> MJ: I could have the students construct their own periodic table. Maybe have them use pictures of the elements, or maybe things that are made of that particular element.
>
> PD: That's a possibility.
>
> MJ: I could have them get into groups and assign several different elements to each group and have them combine them. Or maybe...
>
> PD: Okay. But then all students would only know some of the elements. Didn't you say you want all students to know *all* the elements?
>
> MJ: Yes, that's true.

Through the course of conversation, the professional developer allows the teacher to build on the conversation and talk out her ideas. The professional developer plays off the teacher's ideas, asking further questions and riding out all possible ideas so that the teacher can come to her own understanding of what is an ideal set of strategies. To facilitate the consultation, the professional developer suggests other possibilities:

> PD: What if you used a metaphor for the periodic table? Like, something that the students already knew that could help them conceptualize the table?
>
> MJ: Yes. Something simple, like the alphabet.
>
> PD: That sounds interesting. Can you explain further?
>
> MJ: Well, they are both symbol systems and in the case of both, not every symbol can be combined with every other symbol.
>
> PD: That sounds like a great way to get them to understand the table and begin to learn what elements can be combined with others.

The professional developer suggests—or redesigns—a curriculum approach and allows the teacher to discover the implications of that suggestion. Eventually, the conversation progresses so that both teacher and professional developer tease out the conceptual connections between the alphabet and the periodic table of elements.

MJ: Maybe I could get students to combine the elements, like they were making words out of letters.
PD: An interesting lesson in grammar.
MJ: How could I do that?
PD: Well, it sounds like you are talking about overlaying two symbol systems. We could think of this "interface" in terms of conceptual relations—what elements combine with others. You could create a periodic table in Hyperstudio, for example, and have students create conceptual links among elements. Each element could be a "card" within a "stack" and linked to each card would be concepts related to that element, such as, its atomic weight, what it combines with to form a particular molecule, etc.
MJ: Yes. I think the key is asking students to think conceptually of and within each element. Does that make sense?
PD: I think so. But maybe you'd better explain it to me one more time.

Although the professional developer understands the curriculum challenge as one of overlaying symbol systems, with the periodic table essentially as an interface between symbols and meaning, she must help the teacher to understand those ideas and discover their implications. The professional developer presents herself as a co-learner and nonexpert and opens up the conversation, engaging the teacher in reflective thought about the possibilities for curricular design. As illustrated through the excerpts above, the conversation was primarily philosophical and pedagogical in design. Only towards the end of the conversation did talk emerge about the actual technology. The postponement of tech talk is imperative to the thoughtful and critical uses of technology to support curriculum and teaching.

Ideally, the teacher's goals should include pertinent local, state, and national curriculum standards. An added dimension is

the purpose and passion of the teacher: What (s)he is passionate about, the depths of his/her knowledge, and what (s)he thinks is the most important knowledge for students to create. A central question to ask is: "How can your goals and strategies for achieving those goals be best supported?" It may be that the newest or the highest technology does not necessarily align directly with a teacher's strategies or goals—an important disconnection to discover.

Establishing a Curriculum Goal

Integrating technology across the curriculum implies that our purposes for both technology and education have already been established. As educators, we cannot ignore that our purposes for both are, to a large extent, driven by policies and practices at the local, state, and national levels. It is, therefore, essential that educators become well versed in the various standards and goals that exist. National and state standards, district goals, school goals, and annual themes all anchor curriculum. What are some of your goals for students? A professional developer, or a member of the professional learning community, can guide teachers down the ladder of abstraction, unpacking **eduspeak** that calls for *life-long learning*, *critical thinking*, and/or *participatory citizenship*, for example. Arriving at a goal is a challenge, given the vagueness of eduspeak as well as the distraction created by the desire or presence of newly acquired technologies.

Eduspeak refers to the incomprehensible jargon within the profession of education.

Ideally, the curriculum goal statement should be grounded in a specific content area. The goal should also align with district or school goals, often represented through a yearly theme or mission such as "Caring Communities" or "Reach for the Stars" or even an immediate pressing need such as raising math test scores. At the same time, the curriculum goal should be broadly crafted (e.g., enhance students' reading skills, develop students' understanding of physics). A teacher can also derive a goal statement from specific grade-level strands of standards, such as increasing first-grade students' understanding of weather.

Although the curriculum goal is initially very broad, the next step is to operationally define it through national, state, and local curriculum standards. This is, in many ways, an interpretive exercise. The professional developer then asks teachers to make a list of their selected core content standards that define their

overarching curriculum goal. One teacher chose the goal of "increasing fourth-grade students' proficiency in U.S. geography" and further defined it through the social studies and language arts standards, which include understanding the locations of major geographical, physical, and human characteristics of the United States and reading a variety of materials and texts, using visual information, and writing in clear language. Ultimately, the ways of defining a curriculum goal are numerous and depend upon the extent to which teachers collaborate across disciplines and heed the emergent needs of their school or grade level.

Identifying Teaching Strategies

For better or for worse, most teachers already know how they like to teach and how they want students to learn. Unfortunately, when asked to articulate their strategies for teaching, teachers often respond by explaining the learning products (e.g., quiz, essay, presentation, movie) rather than the processes that will take students to those destinations. The aim at this point in the discussion becomes making explicit the importance of a student-centered pedagogy that directly supports the educational goal. The pedagogical strategies might involve students working in teams, conducting individual research, engaging in large group discussions, making an oral presentation, or engaging in peer critiques. More teacher-centered strategies include lecturing to students, demonstrating a process, guiding a discussion, and posing questions to students. It is important for teachers to identify which of their pedagogical strategies are predominantly teacher-centered and those that are primarily student-centered.

Creating a list of teaching strategies allows teachers to reflect and, if necessary, revise their teaching style to accommodate specific standards and students with special needs. This is an important step, as it emphasizes the significance of how learning occurs, not just what or how information is transmitted. This exercise leads to important conversations about how the methods and media of instruction ultimately shape the curriculum that is enacted in the classroom environment. Because the information literacy and technology literacy standards comprise a perspective or lens for core curriculum content, they serve as a bridge between specific technologies and methods of teaching. In other words, these standards should not comprise the initial curriculum goal;

rather, they should shape the selection of pedagogical strategies. For example, the American Library Association's Information Literacy Standard I refers to accessing information efficiently and effectively. Students in history grades 7–8 should know different types of primary and secondary sources and the motives, interests, and bias expressed in them (e.g., eyewitness accounts, letters, diaries, artifacts, photos, magazine articles, newspaper accounts, hearsay). Similarly, the National Educational Standards for students in grades 3–5 require them to determine when technology is useful and to select the appropriate tool(s) and resources to address a variety of tasks and problems. These technical standards and skills are more appropriate to discuss *after* choosing a curriculum goal, as they often imply methods and specific technology resources for achieving the content goal.

Separating the components of teaching from technology breaks the process of integrating curriculum and technology into manageable parts, similar to an equation (Goals = Strategies + Technologies). Creating a three-columned list of goals/standards, strategies, and technologies ensures that the educational goal is prerequisite to the selection of the technology.

Integration as Alignment

The selection of specific technological tools is contingent upon the ways in which they can directly support specific teaching strategies. Similarly, the selection of teaching strategies is contingent upon the degree to which they help achieve the selected curriculum standards. The technologies, strategies, and goals can be visualized as three columns that serve as a starting point for a curriculum-planning matrix. The number of rows in the matrix is determined by the timeframe for accomplishing the curriculum goal(s). Be it a curriculum unit, module, or marking period, teachers should establish realistic parameters at this point. One possibility is to base the timeframe according to the phases that comprise media literacy (i.e., access, analyze, evaluate, produce, and communicate). Teachers might also use each phase as a benchmark for formalized assessment, as determined by each teacher and the realities of his or her grade level and subject area. Be it a standardized test or a project-based learning, for example, all formal and informal assessments should be clearly indicated within the strategies column as mechanisms for achieving the curriculum goal.

The process of filling in the matrix is a recursive one, and it involves critical questions about how standards are achieved and what teaching strategies and assessments actually support student achievement of curriculum standards. Finally, teachers choose from their technology inventory (see Chapter 4) those items that will support each teaching strategy or a set of strategies. For example, internet access will support teacher demonstration as well as student research. This step clearly requires not only knowledge about how the technologies work, but also knowledge about what each technology enables (and disables) pedagogically. For example, the teacher's use of a presentation will visually supplement a lecture or explanation; however, the technology will not facilitate a class discussion (teachers and students must do that). Similarly, a student's assembly of a presentation does not necessarily display his/her research skills or ability to analyze information. It can, however, demonstrate technological proficiency and display interpretation and understanding of ideas or events. This important step of connecting the dots with technology is an important one, as it sheds light on the benefits and constraints of technologies that may dominate education and yet be of little pedagogical value.

The key to achieving alignment across technologies, strategies, and goals is to readily identify any gaps or inconsistencies across columns and then adjust strategies and technologies accordingly. Achieving alignment can be thought of as creating a set of equations: Technologies + teaching strategies/methods = standards achievement. It is during this process of alignment that teachers often realize that the technologies and even the assessments used are misaligned with their chosen teaching strategies and standards. They may also find that their assessments are not accurately measuring or accounting for student achievement in the chosen area of content standards.

This exercise is a useful anchor for in-service teachers to experiment using new media technologies to support existing curriculum or, conversely, using traditional media technologies to support new or unfamiliar curriculum standards. Once a matrix is established for a particular goal, it provides breadth and depth to curriculum and direction for technology use. It can also ensure that teachers engage students in the entire cycle of media literacy—that students don't just access and analyze information

but also produce and communicate using a variety of skills and technologies.

A Portrait of Integration

My first experiences with reflectively practicing curriculum and technology integration occurred in the late 1990s when I was assigned for eight weeks as a co-teacher of a seventh-grade social studies teacher at an alternative middle school in New York City. During this time, Mayor Giuliani had inundated (at least theoretically) classrooms with computers and E-rate had just gone into effect, although schools at best had one internet connection—usually in the library or the computer lab. Teachers were struggling with what (if anything) to do with computers and were paralyzed in terms of how to begin using them in their curriculum. My co-teacher, Jane, was in her first year of teaching and juggling the challenges of learning state curriculum standards and managing a classroom of 27 highly social adolescents. Jane was responsible for the social studies curriculum piece, and although I was responsible for helping her integrate technology to support her social studies curriculum, we both were open to learning from one another and were open to collaboration, not just cooperation.

I came to the teaching partnership knowing that school administrators defined "technology integration" narrowly (e.g., using computers) and broadly (e.g., for anything classroom-related). So, I was not surprised when Jane initially articulated her goal as getting students to use the six computers in the back of her classroom for some type of project. I gladly supported her desire, knowing that at some point I wanted Jane to recognize on her own the subordinate role of those computers in relation to her curricular goals. Rather than discuss cables, software, and wiring, I continually shifted our initial conversations to Jane's area of expertise and asked questions about what it is that she wanted students to learn. I was both amazed and impressed by her approach to curriculum.

Jane chose the Reconstruction period in the United States as our content area. She felt that historical timelines were helpful in terms of understanding the chronology of events, but they did not help students to understand history to the meaningful extent she wanted. She understood history to be a complex interplay of people and events, with rarely only one true story as textbooks

had a tendency to promote. For example, Jane pointed out that the Reconstruction began in 1863, although the Civil War did not officially end until 1865, and required narrative explanations that addressed multiple perspectives. I encouraged Jane to pay particular attention in her course preparation to the ways in which the Reconstruction period (and history in general) is mediated through political speeches, original documents, political cartoons, photography, diaries, and illustrations and, therefore, construct historical meaning.

Another important question I asked Jane prior to discussing any use of computer technology was, "What do the state standards mandate for this subject area?" We found that the New York State Curriculum frameworks for social studies required an analysis of the post–Civil War Reconstruction (1850 to 1877) to "explore the ideas embodied" in historical documents. Students should "recognize the connections and interactions of people and events across time from a variety of perspectives." As part of making connections, the standards suggested that students investigate from a variety of sources and identify varying points of view. It also recommended that students undertake case studies and engage in mapping exercises, and that they use photographs and interviews, newspaper accounts, and other sources. Most importantly, I found elements embedded within the frameworks that are foundational to media literacy:

> Effective [civic] participation is rooted in the ability to make informed judgments on issues that have confronted and continue to confront American society. Students learn to summarize accurately points of view on issues, distinguish between relevant and irrelevant data, analyze arguments, and weigh evidence before taking positions and making judgments.

As we wrote down our curriculum content goals for the course, Jane found most interesting that the Reconstruction period raised issues about government and the rights of citizens that remained long after 1877. She was fascinated with the idea that debate over the rightful power of the federal government and the states continues to the present, as Americans continue to wrestle with the problem of providing civil rights and equal opportunity to all citizens. Jane wanted to go in-depth into how the above issues were approached during the Reconstruction period and have students find connections between the past and the present. She liked the idea of framing the course in terms of students as both researchers and investigative reporters who are assigned the task of gathering media resources to tell the story of the Reconstruction from multiple perspectives: political, economic, social, and cultural. Thus, the main question we came up with to guide the course was: "How did the events of the Reconstruction influence (and were influenced by) the events that proceeded/followed it?" Jane constructed a set of focused questions to guide students in their research:

> Political: Who held power locally? Statewide?
> Federal? What political organizations were active
> during the Reconstruction?
> Economic: What was the economy like? Who had
> the jobs? How much did things cost? Look at the
> connections between class and political/social status.
> What images were on money? On Confederate
> money?
> Social: How were people living during this time?
> What were the conditions in the North? The South?
> How did people interact?
> Cultural: What were the representations of the time
> in the press? In photographs? Art? Theatre? Music?
> Dance? How did religious views play a role in the
> Reconstruction?

Only after intense discussions about what the students should know about the Reconstruction, did I entertain discussions about how they should learn and then represent what they learned. Jane had already decided she wanted students to use the six computers in the back of her room. Since she had no internet access in her classroom, we decided that students would construct (produce) their own representations of their understanding of the Reconstruction. She liked the idea of students "rewriting" history with multimedia. At the very least, Jane wanted them to use images and text to tell their stories. In exploring some of the software options, we decided that in her situation, the most accessible (inexpensive) and easy-to-use software program was Hyperstudio, a software program that operates on the metaphor of a stack of cards. The "cards" could be interconnected through hyperlinks and it was possible to combine multimedia forms (e.g., text, sound, images, animation) on each card. Unlike a book, there was no "first" page. Thus, the connections among card contents

become of paramount importance—similar to the importance of the connections among the political, economic, social, and cultural perspectives of the Reconstruction period. The nonlinear design of Hyperstudio supported well Jane's nonlinear view of history.

In thinking how to assess this final product of the course, Jane and I equally weighted group participation, planning and research, and stack design. Class participation and Hyperstudio stack content together would comprise 50 percent of the project grade. Jane wanted to see students express their understanding of their specific topic through the use of factual, interesting, and relevant information. Most of the written text on each card had to consist of original thought and was required to contain political, economic, social, and cultural dimensions of the topic. Jane also privileged the ability of these seventh graders to complete class activities and assignments and to work considerately and efficiently with group members. Research and planning along with stack design (connections) comprised 40 percent of the project grade. We required the students to complete a "research agenda" to guide their group work and to complete a card-planning sheet before each Hyperstudio production session. Their stacks required a minimum of 10 cards, including a title card, bibliography, and "credits" card; 10 percent of the points were allotted for creativity.

We designed the course as an eight-week module that met three days a week for a block period. We thought of the eight weeks as a progression requiring a series of scaffolding events and assignments to generate media resources for the assignment and to also prepare students' thinking about nonlinear conceptual design. To ensure sufficient time for the entire (media literacy) cycle of student access, analysis, evaluation, and production, Jane chose to gather printed information from newspapers, textbooks, museums, and historical societies to supply students in class with a bank of information to select from and build their research on. Students would select pieces of information and write journal entries to analyze and reflect upon their significance. Additional resources available to students were magazines, TV, film, the internet, letters, and people. Each week, each group analyzed the four dimensions of the topic for that week via media sources and create a collage above and below the timeline on the wall in front of the classroom. At the end of the six weeks, the group makes the final decisions as to what to keep in their construction of the Reconstruction through Hyperstudio and what to add.

The first two weeks were devoted to laying the groundwork in terms of both the Reconstruction and a media literacy framework. Our progression began with a visual literacy exercise on the topic of Abraham Lincoln. We asked students to look at a series of political cartoons and illustrations of Lincoln in different contexts. We asked the students to write about what they actually saw in each picture and then what they inferred or assumed, based on what they saw. The goal was to get each student to identify the language of the medium (cartoon drawings) to tell the story of the image and then have the class discuss how the language of the cartoons constructed a particular meaning. We then discussed how they, as readers, interpreted the symbols and how they arrived at their (different) interpretations. We then contextualized historically the symbols within the cartoon and discussed its historical meaning. We led students through a similar exercise with a painting portrait of Lincoln and asked how it is similar to/different from the cartoon. The students identified the portrait as portraying Lincoln upright, in comparison to a "demonizing" look in the cartoon. The class identified Lincoln as regal and calm in the painting and frustrated and peasant-like in the cartoon. Jane followed this exercise with a mini-lecture on how Lincoln viewed his own experiences, using his historical writings. We then asked the class to draw their own portrait of Lincoln, "What would Lincoln's self-portrait look like, based on what we know from his writings?" Another homework assignment involved creating a cartoon of Lincoln titled "Writing the Emancipation Proclamation." Students were required to include several symbols reflecting their own understanding of what went into Lincoln's thinking when he was writing the Emancipation Proclamation. The students were also required to include a short essay accompanying the cartoon that explained what their symbols represented. Students presented these cartoons in class and read their essays. The presentations ended with a brief discussion beyond the classroom context: "In what other situations besides cartoons and paintings do you regularly interpret pictures?" They mentioned newspapers, billboards, magazine ads, menus, photo albums, and class pictures.

At the end of the third week, Jane felt the students knew enough about the Reconstruction period to choose topics for their media production project. She mentioned that although she would ideally like to facilitate a class discussion of the most important issues of the time period and have students generate their own list of topics, she decided to generate her own list of topics that taken together comprised a comprehensive list of Reconstruction topics: Constitutional amendments, Southern resistance, federal government, social and political advances for African Americans, and Northerners come South. Jane also felt strongly about providing her students with as many opportunities to personalize history and to connect historical events with their own lives as young people living in New York City. The entire class visited a Reconstruction exhibit at the local Schomburg Museum. Students completed a worksheet during their visit that asked them to "tell the story" of the object they selected and to describe specifically how the arrangement, color, and textual description of the exhibit helped them construct the story of their object. How do your particular interests and experiences influence the way in which you interpret this exhibit? What values does it express? On the backs of their worksheets, students were asked to design and sketch (while still in the museum) one Hyperstudio card, based on what they learned about their artifact at the museum and think about how it connected to their group topic.

We also showed the video "Facing History" and co-facilitated a class discussion about the artistic construction of black history. We then asked students to construct a collage to represent the Reconstruction in light of their specific topic. This not only gave students practice in expressing their understanding of history through creating an original piece of artwork but also provided an opportunity to engage in reflection about history as a construction as well as about the medium of instruction (the video itself) as constructing history curriculum.

As students gathered content for their presentation, I facilitated their (re)production of it. Weeks three through six involved breaking the class into two groups: Jane working with one half of the students to explain the major tenets from the post–Civil War Reconstruction period (e.g., how the government works, branches of government and the Constitutional amendments) while I tutored the other half of the class in the computer lab on how to use Hyperstudio. About one-third of the class of students already knew the technical features of Hyperstudio. Regardless, we split the class in half and I taught each group Hyperstudio within the school computer lab during the third week of the module. In order for the students' knowledge of this nonlinear multimedia program to be useful in the future, they needed to understand how Hyperstudio worked conceptually. So, I guided them through a nonlinear mapping exercise as a precursor to connecting the stacks. I gave each group of students a big sheet of paper to draw on. I asked them to map out the process of going to the movies. They soon learned that illustrating that topic is not a linear process, but rather they have to decide within their group what movie to see, where the movie is playing, if they have money, and other aspects of the plan. This exercise segued into asking them to map out how their subtopics on the Reconstruction interconnect.

The culmination of the project was in the students making points of connection among history and among Hyperstudio stacks during the seventh week of the course. Each group presented to the rest of the class their stack of their particular Reconstruction topic. After all the groups made their presentations, the entire class deliberated on how their stacks interconnected (touching upon the nonlinear interaction of historical events). To preserve time for student reflection, we did not have students make the technical connections among their stacks as they had already mastered the technical skill. Instead, we cleared the desks from the classroom and placed printouts of all the stacks across the floor. With a big role of masking tape, the students walked around and made physical connections among stacks.

Week eight involved a written "final exam" that asked students to reflect on what they had learned about the Reconstruction and about the technology of Hyperstudio as a means to understanding the Reconstruction. Jane and I felt strongly that after all the chaos of the preceding weeks, students needed to gain some distance from their projects to be able to reflect on their work in a meaningful way. We asked students to collectively write a Hyperstudio "manual" including critical strategies for beginners. Some of their suggestions included: "Always have a button going to your home card because you can get lost in other stacks or cards," "Always plan out your card before

you put it on your card on Hyperstudio." Their project-based experience with the software enabled them to command the technology, rather than feel subjected to it. These students were able to see the mediation of history through perspectives of various media forms: textbooks, political cartoons, films, original documents, and a museum exhibit. Most importantly, they were able to use the languages of multimedia to (re)write history from a critical perspective.

This "Constructing the Reconstruction" project breaks the boundaries of the traditional 40-minute classroom period and the monopoly of print materials within schooling. On a pedagogical level, Jane learned that her role was not limited to technological skill building and information delivery. She experienced the integration of computer technology into her curriculum as accomplishing more than providing students with a technical skill set. From a critical-interpretive standpoint, this social studies module facilitated democracy, creativity, and transformative knowledge among this group of seventh graders. Other teachers who are interested in a critical approach to technology should ask, "Am I sensitizing students to think critically about information? To interact socially? To value orality? To transform knowledge, rather than acquire it?" Learning is an ongoing conversation in which history, assumptions, prejudices, and knowledge are continually (re)examined. Such a pedagogy is rewarding, yet challenging. It requires teachers to keep the conversation going among students' interpretations and reactions, the media texts and technologies, and their creators.

As students become producers of media, not just users of technology, they become producers within and of their communities and environments in which they live. Responsibilities for access to knowledge and technologies are, therefore, a shared responsibility of the families and communities in which students live. The purpose of the classroom then shifts to that of a space for reflection and dialogue about media experiences and their meanings. Ideally, the classroom should be a safe haven for experimentation, reflection, and renewal of ideas and ideals before students return to their transformative roles within their communities. The potential of media technologies, both old and new, lies in the facilitation of dialogue that can bridge the chasms of diversity. Media literacy is the turnkey to integrating technology

into classroom curricula in meaningful and socially responsible ways. It empowers students to make choices about how and when (and whether) to use technologies as a means to social and political ends.

Professional development is an integral part of curriculum and technology integration. Teachers are professionals who have the capacity to transform their teaching and technological practices in a generative fashion, over time. Teacher professional development must also enable and support teacher inquiry into subject matter, student learning, and teaching practice, so that teachers can adapt their practices in ways appropriate to the demands of subject matter and their students' learning.

Toward a Pedagogy of Communification

To integrate technological, communication, and educational processes and products is indeed a complex challenge. The convergence of the various facets of technology discussed in this book results in what I call a pedagogy of **communification**. In its broadest sense, communification implies the integration of communication, education, and technological processes and products to convene diverse groups of people who achieve interdependence through a shared vision and common goal. Communification requires technology in all its forms to serve schooling in ways that are communicative, unifying, and communal. In other words, the ultimate value of technology in schools will be measured according to its capacity to satisfy the human need to communicate, commune, and connect with others in order to (re)construct the world around them.

Communification is the use of various communication media and technologies to achieve communal and unifying experiences among diverse groups of people.

Human communication is paramount. An essential goal of communification is to achieve a deep understanding of both human communication and technologies, to locate the ways in which technology-mediated communication shapes social, political, and economic practices. Although high-speed wireless networks inarguably pose many great possibilities and hope for bridging educational and cultural gaps across the world, the loss of orality and human contact present serious challenges that greatly effect millions of young people going through formal systems of schooling.

The pendulum of history has swung from individualized student learning back to subject matter emphasis. The inability

to reconcile the two is illustrated in the current climate of an "achievement gap" that refers to the disparity in school performance (e.g., grades, test scores, course selection, college completion) according to racial and ethnic differences. The continuous pressure for educators and administrators to keep an eye on the moving target of technological innovation distracts us from what should be of paramount importance to education: The student. Regardless of what medium or technology we choose, whether low-tech or high-tech, our successes as educators will ultimately be measured by our ability (or lack thereof) to communicate effectively in various technologically mediated environments. A pedagogy of communification, therefore, requires teachers to be purposeful, precise, and pragmatic in the selection and uses of technology in their teaching. In other words, we need to continuously inquire why students and teacher convene in a classroom 180 days of the calendar year. Or why groups of "users" convene online. Such efficacy will occur only if educators and students understand the ways in which media and technology characteristics shape human communication.

Educators must also understand that the new literacies associated with technology are primarily discursive (and symbolic) processes of meaning making and are not limited to the acquisition of artifacts and skills identified by corporations as essential for twenty-first-century high school graduates. Political and economic forces have historically driven the technology bandwagon in schools, the most current example being the corporate-saturated *Partnership for 21st Century Skills (P21)* that lobbies for increased communication skills and collaboration. However, the main concern of this consortium (consisting of mostly high-tech businesses and just a few educational organizations) is that U.S. schools are not preparing students with the skills they need to compete in the new global economy. Fear and competition pervade the discourse of many such organizations pushing for increased technology skills. Other countries such as China and India have dramatically improved their education and workforce, fueling concerns that the economic dominance of the United States may be slipping. With the push in the United States to technologically educate "our own" above others, the existence of more technologically mediated communication may actually encourage *less* cultural diversity and less intercultural communication. In contrast, using technology to achieve communification focuses on the interconnection of diverse groups of people so that commonality will emerge. In other words, diversity is not an afterthought, but rather a starting point. Our role as educators must include bringing together diverse groups of people and to interconnect them in ways that are socially, culturally, intellectually, spiritually, and technologically meaningful.

Achieve unification of purpose. Strengthening local communities requires that individuals perceive a shared purpose. U.S. history reveals that the common schools of the nineteenth century resembled missionary work (under the banner of overcoming temporal hardship and promoting a common American identity) more than it resembled academics. Schooling was imbued with the values of pluralism, piety, and productivity in terms of efficiently transmitting knowledge and culture. By contemporary standards, common schools were chaotic, crowded, primitive, and culturally oppressive. Yet they were also powerful communal spaces where immigrant children collectively learned what to believe in and how to behave. In a nation that had experienced violent divisions that culminated in a brutal Civil War, achieving unity of educational purpose was crucial to the role of schools in securing the nation's future. For better or worse, common schools supplied children with a common language and a set of beliefs that unified the immigrant populations struggling to survive within the United States. At this point in the history of schooling, we must stop and rethink the direction and purpose of education in the United States. What are we educating students to know and be able to do? Is schooling in the twenty-first century equipping students to reconstruct the world in socially responsive—and responsible—ways?

Clearly there is an economic purpose for schooling and the uses of technology within those structures: To secure the nation's future. However, it is shortsighted to educate citizenry with mere technical skills, as the federal push for technological literacy suggests. Just as a technician might defragment a hard drive (reorganizing data so that the drive runs more efficiently), educators must similarly "defragment" students' curricular experiences. This includes asking the basic question: "Is this technology necessary in order to achieve our purpose?"

Communification also requires temperance of capitalistic forces that narrow education into the acquisition of facts and skills. The process is similar to a musician moving beyond technical mastery of an instrument to the realm of making music. Students need to move beyond memorization of facts to ultimately think more deeply about ideas and to expand knowledge (i.e., "Could the Civil War happen again?" "What does calculus allow me to do in my daily life?"). This in turn requires a fundamental shift in educators' perceptions of technology and the purposes of schooling: From multiplicity of subjects and devices to a simplicity of ideas and tools; from fragmentation of information (on the web) and factoids in the classroom to a unification of knowledge (via themes or questions).

Educators must also be cautious about corporate-school partnerships, since the relationship denotes that both parties are working towards a common goal. Although a surface glance may suggest that contracts between businesses and schools may be mutually beneficial, the reality is that competition (the opposite of partnership) is the nature of business. Achieving unification within schools and communities is hindered by corporate takeovers and the subsequent management of "failing" schools for purposes that are more bureaucratic than democratic in design and practice. If students have neither school nor home access to technology, technology leaders should first look within the wider educational community: public libraries, community centers, and nonprofit organizations can partner with schools to provide services and access to equipment. Equity of access can be accomplished through combined efforts and seeing that schooling occurs beyond the four walls of the classroom. Ultimately, the greatest benefit technology brings to schooling is the facilitation of experiences that interconnect administrators, teachers, students, experts, communities, families, and policymakers in a continuous renewal of educational purpose(s) for schooling.

Seek communal experiences. Temporal hardships are divided between those suffering extreme poverty and those infected with what de Graaf, Wann, and Naylor (2001) refer to as **affluenza,** a socially transmitted condition characterized by overload, financial debt, anxiety, and waste in the United States. Collateral damage from economic prosperity and rapid technological developments

Affluenza

is a socially transmitted condition characterized by overload, financial debt, anxiety, and waste.

includes excessive individualism and social isolationism as local cities are increasingly segregated along economic and racial lines. Our understanding of others who are different from us is, therefore, less likely to occur through face-to-face interaction and is more likely to be mediated through modern communications technologies (i.e., television, film, internet, cell phones). The paradox of technology lies in the façade of connectivity: Although computer networks allow just about anyone to communicate with just about anyone else in just about any part of the world (language barriers notwithstanding), such technologies do not show us how to build or sustain human relationships. At the root of communification is *commune*, which means to come into close spiritual contact and to share intimate thoughts or feelings with someone or something. In an ideal communal society, everyone works together and the ownership of property and possessions is shared. Rights and responsibilities associated with the social, political, and economic uses of technology are also shared.

The human path of least resistance is to align ourselves with those of similar interests. We don't necessarily seek out those who are different from ourselves. In fact, we seek common ground, as evidenced on the internet as an interest-based medium. How then can we privilege diversity and democracy in such homogeneous circumstances? Surely there is a plethora of opportunity for educators to address the challenges associated with online social networking among young people—to expand students' awareness, knowledge, and respect for others who are different from them. With so much information available via the internet, educators must carefully consider the question, "What is the purpose of the classroom?" It makes little sense to use classroom time for students to sit behind a computer, other than for live technical demonstrations or a formal class presentation.

Communification is achieved when educators, parents, students, and policymakers individually and collectively use technology to engage in practices that show a commitment to the common good, while at the same time privileging diversity. This happens when diverse groups of people commune based on felt needs and/or interests, and not necessarily the interests of corporations or even standardized curriculum.

Education as social (re)construction. What makes a communications technology an *educational* technology is the pedagogical end to which it is employed. The ultimate value of computers, the internet, and other technologies in schools lies in their capacity to strengthen localized communities through their strategic use among students.

And so we arrive at a definition of technology in schools that is neither radical nor conservative. Communification is neither concerned with space nor time. Conceptually it represents a more fluid, holistic, and integrative approach to curriculum, teaching, and technology. Technology leaders can (re)design their curriculum to privilege the classroom primarily as a discursive environment where students commune with one another while other non-classroom contexts serve as environments for individual computing experiences. Rethinking technology in schools requires teacher leaders who: (1) seek to understand their students; (2) seek to understand the communication characteristics associated with technological devices; (3) seek to locate authentic and communal educational purpose; and (4) shift the focus away from mere access to machines or adherence to a particular set of skills. Ultimately, schools require a more holistic and humanistic framework that privileges diversity of all kinds, even technological diversity.

Glossary

Integration—is the combining and coordinating of separate parts or elements into a unified whole. It requires a much more complex orchestration of activities than merely using high-tech devices in schooling.

Constructivism—is a theory of learning based on the idea that humans actively construct their own knowledge based on their own perceptions and understandings.

Eduspeak—refers to the incomprehensible jargon within the profession of education.

Communification—is the use of various communication media and technologies to achieve communal and unifying experiences among diverse groups of people.

Affluenza—is a socially transmitted condition characterized by overload, financial debt, anxiety, and waste.

Appendix A

International Society for Technology in Education (ISTE) National Educational Technology Standards for Students (NETS-S) 2007

I. Creativity and Innovation

Students demonstrate creative thinking, construct knowledge, and develop innovative products and processes using technology. Students:

a. apply existing knowledge to generate new ideas, products, or processes.

b. create original works as a means of personal or group expression.

c. use models and simulations to explore complex systems and issues.

d. identify trends and forecast possibilities.

II. Communication and Collaboration

Students use digital media and environments to communicate and work collaboratively, including at a distance, to support

individual learning and contribute to the learning of others. Students:

a. interact, collaborate, and publish with peers, experts, or others employing a variety of digital environments and media.
b. communicate information and ideas effectively to multiple audiences using a variety of media and formats.
c. develop cultural understanding and global awareness by engaging with learners of other cultures.
d. contribute to project teams to produce original works or solve problems.

III. Research and Information Fluency

Students apply digital tools to gather, evaluate, and use information. Students:

a. plan strategies to guide inquiry.
b. locate, organize, analyze, evaluate, synthesize, and ethically use information from a variety of sources and media.
c. evaluate and select information sources and digital tools based on the appropriateness to specific tasks.
d. process data and report results.

IV. Critical Thinking, Problem Solving, and Decision Making

Students use critical thinking skills to plan and conduct research, manage projects, solve problems, and make informed decisions using appropriate digital tools and resources. Students:

a. identify and define authentic problems and significant questions for investigation.
b. plan and manage activities to develop a solution or complete a project.
c. collect and analyze data to identify solutions and/or make informed decisions.
d. use multiple processes and diverse perspectives to explore alternative solutions.

V. Digital Citizenship

Students understand human, cultural, and societal issues related to technology and practice legal and ethical behavior. Students:

a. advocate and practice safe, legal, and responsible use of information and technology.

b. exhibit a positive attitude toward using technology that supports collaboration, learning, and productivity.

c. demonstrate personal responsibility for lifelong learning.

d. exhibit leadership for digital citizenship.

VI. Technology Operations and Concepts

Students demonstrate a sound understanding of technology concepts, systems, and operations. Students:

a. understand and use technology systems.

b. select and use applications effectively and productively.

c. troubleshoot systems and applications.

d. transfer current knowledge to learning of new technologies.

NETS for Students:

National Educational Technology Standards for Students, Second Edition, (c) 2007, ISTE(r) (International Society for Technology in Education), www.iste.org. All rights reserved.

Appendix B

International Society for Technology in Education (ISTE) National Educational Technology Standards for Teachers (NETS-T) 2008

I. Facilitate and Inspire Student Learning and Creativity

Teachers use their knowledge of subject matter, teaching and learning, and technology to facilitate experiences that advance student learning, creativity, and innovation in both face-to-face and virtual environments. Teachers:

a. promote, support, and model creative and innovative thinking and inventiveness.

b. engage students in exploring real-world issues and solving authentic problems using digital tools and resources.

c. promote student reflection using collaborative tools to reveal and clarify students' conceptual understanding and thinking, planning, and creative processes.

d. model collaborative knowledge construction by engaging in learning with students, colleagues, and others in face-to-face and virtual environments.

II. Design and Develop Digital-Age Learning Experiences and Assessments

Teachers design, develop, and evaluate authentic learning experiences and assessment incorporating contemporary tools and resources to maximize content learning in context and to develop the knowledge, skills, and attitudes identified in the NETS-S. Teachers:

a. design or adapt relevant learning experiences that incorporate digital tools and resources to promote student learning and creativity.

b. develop technology-enriched learning environments that enable all students to pursue their individual curiosities and become active participants in setting their own educational goals, managing their own learning, and assessing their own progress.

c. customize and personalize learning activities to address students' diverse learning styles, working strategies, and abilities using digital tools and resources.

d. provide students with multiple and varied formative and summative assessments aligned with content and technology standards and use resulting data to inform learning and teaching.

III. Model Digital-Age Work and Learning

Teachers exhibit knowledge, skills, and work processes representative of an innovative professional in a global and digital society. Teachers:

a. demonstrate fluency in technology systems and the transfer of current knowledge to new technologies and situations.

b. collaborate with students, peers, parents, and community members using digital tools and resources to support student success and innovation.

c. communicate relevant information and ideas effectively to students, parents, and peers using a variety of digital-age media and formats.

d. model and facilitate effective use of current and emerging digital tools to locate, analyze, evaluate, and use information resources to support research and learning.

IV. Promote and Model Digital Citizenship and Responsibility

Teachers understand local and global societal issues and responsibilities in an evolving digital culture and exhibit legal and ethical behavior in their professional practices. Teachers:

a. advocate, model, and teach safe, legal, and ethical use of digital information and technology, including respect for copyright, intellectual property, and the appropriate documentation of sources.

b. address the diverse needs of all learners by using learner-centered strategies providing equitable access to appropriate digital tools and resources.

c. promote and model digital etiquette and responsible social interactions related to the use of technology and information.

d. develop and model cultural understanding and global awareness by engaging with colleagues and students of other cultures using digital-age communication and collaboration tools.

V. Engage in Professional Growth and Leadership

Teachers continuously improve their professional practice, model lifelong learning, and exhibit leadership in their school and professional community by promoting and demonstrating the effective use of digital tools and resources. Teachers:

a. participate in local and global learning communities to explore creative applications of technology to improve student learning.

b. exhibit leadership by demonstrating a vision of technology infusion, participating in shared decision making and community building, and developing the leadership and technology skills of others.

c. evaluate and reflect on current research and professional practice on a regular basis to make effective use of existing and emerging digital tools and resources in support of student learning.

d. contribute to the effectiveness, vitality, and self-renewal of the teaching profession and of their school and community.

NETS for Teachers:

National Educational Technology Standards for Teachers, Second Edition (c) 2008 ISTE (r) (International Society for Technology in Education), www.iste.org. All rights reserved.

Bibliography and Resources

Addicott, I. O. (1939). *A study of the nature and elementary school use of free printed matter prepared as advertising media.* Unpublished doctoral dissertation, School of Education, Leland Stanford Junior University, Stanford, California.

Adelson, J. (1972). The political imagination of the young adolescent. In J. Kagan & R. Coles (Eds.). *Twelve to sixteen: Early adolescence* (pp. 106–143). New York: W. W. Norton.

American Association of School Librarians (AASL), & Association for Educational Communications and Technology (AECT). (1998). *Information power: Building partnerships for learning.* Chicago: American Library Association.

American Democracy Project (2003). Civic engagement, higher education, and the 21st century. A cooperative project of the American Association of State Colleges and Universities (AASCU), *The New York Times,* and AASCU member-institutions. Retrieved November 20, 2007 from http://www.indiana.edu/ idsa/diversity/ADPproposal.pdf.

American Educational Research Association (AERA). (2005). Teaching teachers: Professional development to improve student achievement. *TechPoints: Essential Information for Education Policy, 3*(1), 1–4.

Anderson, L. S. (2005, November). A digital doorway to the world. *T.H.E. Journal,* 14–16.

Apple, M. W. (1990). *Ideology and curriculum* (2nd ed.). New York: Routledge.

Armsey, J. W., & Dahl, N. C. (1973). *An inquiry into the uses of instructional technology*. New York: Ford Foundation.

Asthana, S. (2006). *Innovative practices of youth participation in media*. Paris: United Nations Educational, Scientific and Cultural Organization (UNESCO).

Aufderheide, P. (1993). *Media literacy: A report of the National Leadership Conference on Media Literacy*. Washington, DC: Aspen Institute.

Ayars, A. L. (1964, October 17). How business and industry are helping the schools. *Saturday Review, 47*(42), 57–71.

Baggott, K. (2006, December 21). Literacy and text messaging: How will the next generation read and write? *Technology Review*. Retrieved January 4, 2007 from http://www.technologyreview.com/printer_friendly_article.aspx?id=17927.

Bandura, A. (1971). *Psychological modeling: Conflicting theories*. Chicago: Aldine-Atherton.

Barker, G. (2006). Big rap for tiny music machine. *The Age*. Retrieved November 15, 2006 from http://www.theage.com/au/news/technology/big-rap-for-tiny-music-machine/2006/11/03/1162340056138.html.

Bazalgette, C. (1991). *Media education*. London: Hodder & Stoughton.

Beane, J. A., & Apple, M. W. (1995). The case for democratic schools. In M. W. Apple & J. A. Beane (Eds.). *Democratic schools* (pp. 1–25). Alexandria, VA: Association for Supervision and Curriculum Development.

Bell, L. (2001). Preparing tomorrow's teachers to use technology: Perspectives of the leaders of twelve national education associations. *Contemporary Issues in Technology and Teacher Education, 1*(4), 517–534.

Bennett, W. L. (Ed.). (2007). *Civic life online: Learning how digital media can engage youth*. Cambridge, MA: MIT Press.

Benton Foundation. (1997). The learning connection: Schools in the information age. Washington, DC: Benton Foundation. Retrieved July 13, 2006 from http://www.benton.org/publibrary/schools/connection.html.

Berger, P. L., & Luckman, T. (1966). *The social construction of reality: A treatise in the sociology of knowledge*. New York: Doubleday.

Berman, S. (1997). *Children's social consciousness and the development of social responsibility*. New York: SUNY Press.

Blane, D. (2006, January 27). The pod people. *The Times Educational Supplement*, p. 21. Retrieved January 4, 2007 from http://www.tes.co.uk/search/story/?story_id=2187080.

Bleimes, A. (2006, November 15). Blogging now begins young. *USA Today*. Retrieved November 15, 2006 from http://news.yahoo.com/s/usatoday/20061115/ tc_usatoday/bloggingnowbeginsyoung.

Blumer, H. (1969). *Symbolic interactionism*. Englewood Cliffs, NJ: Prentice-Hall.

Borja, R. R. (2006a, October 11). Social-networking sites for schools promote safety, education benefits. *Education Week*. Retrieved October 11, 2006 from http://www.edweek.org/ew/articles/2006/10/11/07newtork.h26.html.

Borja, R. R. (2006b, October 25). Technology upgrades prompt schools to go wireless. *Education Week*. Retrieved October 25, 2006 from http://www.edweek.org/ew/articles/2006/10/25/09wireless.h26.htm.

Bowers, C. A. (1998). The paradox of technology: What's gained and lost? *Thought and Action, 14*(1), 49–57.

Bowles, S., & Gintis, H. (1976). *Schooling in capitalist America: Educational reform and the contradictions of economic life*. New York: Basic Books.

Broome, E. C. (1929). Report of the Committee on Propaganda in the Schools. Paper presented at the annual meeting of the National Education Association, Atlanta, GA.

Bruner, J. S. (1986). *Actual minds, possible worlds*. Cambridge: Harvard University Press.

Bruner, J., & Haste, H. (Eds.). (1987). *Making sense: The child's construction of the world*. London: Methuen.

Brunner, C., & Tally, W. (1999). *The new media literacy handbook: An educator's guide to bringing new media into the classroom*. New York: Anchor Books.

Buckingham, D. (1993a). *Children talking television: The making of television literacy*. London: Falmer Press.

Buckingham, D. (Ed.). (1993b). *Reading audiences: Young people and the media* (pp. 1–23). New York: St. Martin's Press.

Buckingham, D. (1996). *Moving images: Understanding children's emotional responses to television.* Manchester: Manchester University Press.

Buckingham, D. (2000a). *After the death of childhood: Growing up in the age of electronic media*. Cambridge: Polity Press.

Buckingham, D. (2000b). *The making of citizens: Young people, news and politics*. London: Routledge.

Burniske, R. W., & Monke, L. (2001). *Breaking down the digital walls: Learning to teach in a post-modem world*. New York: SUNY Press.

Burst Media Corporation (2006, May). Teens online. Online Insights, 6(4). Retrieved July 11, 2006 from http://www.burstmedia.com/assets/newsletter/items/2006_05_01.pdf.

Callahan, R. E. (1962). *Education and the cult of efficiency*. Chicago: University of Chicago Press.

Campbell, G. (2005). There's something in the air: Podcasting in education. *EDUCAUSE Review, 40*(6), 32–47.

Carroll, J. S., & Miller, R. B. (1935, October). The Carroll-Miller list of teaching aids and educational materials from commercial sources. *California Department of Education Bulletin*, 20.

Carter, G. (2002). Laboratories of democracy: The public mission of our nation's schools. *Is it good for the kids?* Association for Supervision and Curriculum Development. Retrieved December 5, 2002 from http://www.ascd.org/educationnews/kids/kids052002.html

Center for Media Education (CME). (1996). "And now a web from our sponsor:" How online advertisers are cashing in on children. *InfoActive*, 2(2), 1–10. Washington, DC: Center for Media Education.

Center for Media Education (CME). (1997). New report documents threats to youth from alcohol and tobacco web sites. Retrieved December 15, 1997 from http://tap.epn.org/cme/pr970306.html.

Center for Public Broadcasting. (1998). Study of school uses of television and video: 1996–1997. Retrieved December 9, 1998 from http://www.cpb.org/library/schoolusestudy/index.html.

Center for Information and Research on Civic Learning and Engagement (CIRCLE). (2006). *The 2006 civic and political health of the nation: A detailed look at how youth participate in politics and communities*. Retrieved November 20, 2007 from http://www.civicyouth.org/PopUps/2006_CPHS_Report_update.pdf.

CEO Forum on Education and Technology. (2001, June). *The CEO Forum school technology and readiness report: Key building blocks for student achievement in the 21st century*. Retrieved February 21, 2002 from http://www.ceoforum.org/downloads/report4.pdf.

Chester, J. (2007). *Digital destiny: New media and the future of democracy*. New York: New Press.

Cleeland, N. (2006, July 23). Rich, poor live poles apart in L. A. as middle class keeps shrinking. *Los Angeles Times*. Retrieved July 24, 2006 from http://www.latimes.com/news/local/.

Cobb, P., & McClain, K. (2001). The collective mediation of a high-stakes accountability program: Communities and networks of practice. In E. Kelly & R. Lesh (Eds.), *Design research in mathematics and science education*. Mahwah, NJ: Erlbaum.

Committee on Consumer Relations in Advertising. (1945). *The 1945 catalog of business-sponsored educational materials*. New York: Committee on Consumer Relations in Advertising.

Condit, L. (1939). *A pamphlet about pamphlets*. Chicago: University of Chicago Press.

Consumers Union Education Services (CUES). (1995). *Captive kids: Commercial pressures on kids at school*. New York: CUES.

A cool partnership established. *Curriculum Review*, 46(5), 9.

Copps, M. J. (2006, June 7). Remarks of Commissioner Michael J. Copps. *Beyond censorship: Technologies and policies to give parents control over children's media*

content. Washington, DC. Kaiser Family Foundation/New America Foundation. Retrieved November 1, 2007 from http://hraunfoss.fcc. gov/edocs_public/attachmatch/DOC-265842A1.pdf

Cross, J., O'Driscoll, T., & Trondsen, R. (2007). Another life: Virtual worlds as tools for learning. *eLearn Magazine.* Retrieved March 26, 2007 from http://elearnmag.org/subpage.cfm?section=articles&article=44-1

Cuban, L. (1986). *Teachers and machines: The classroom use of technology since 1920.* New York: Teachers College Press.

Culp, K. M., Honey, M., & Mandinach, E. (2003, October). *A retrospective on twenty years of education technology policy.* New York: Education Development Center, Center for Children and Technology.

Darling-Hammond, L. (1999). *Teacher quality and student achievement: A review of state policy evidence.* Seattle, WA: University of Washington Center for Teaching Policy.

DeBell, M., & Chapman, C. (2003). *Computer and internet use by children and adolescents in the United States, 2001.* Washington, DC: National Center for Education Statistics. NCES 2004–2014.

DeBell, M., & Chapman, C. (2005). *Rates of computer and internet use by children in nursery school and students in kindergarten through twelfth grade, 2003.* Washington, DC: National Center for Education Statistics. NCES 2005–2111.

de Graaf, J., Wann, D., & Naylor, T. H. (2001). *Affluenza: The all-consuming epidemic.* San Francisco: Berrett-Koehler Publishers.

Dennis, E. E., & LaMay, C. L. (Eds.). (1993). *America's schools and the mass media.* New Brunswick, NJ: Transaction Publishers.

Denzin, N. (1992). *Symbolic interactionism and cultural studies: The politics of interpretation.* Oxford: Blackwell.

Dewey, J. (1897). *My pedagogical creed.* New York: E. L. Kellogg & Company.

Dewey, J. (1916). *Democracy and education: An introduction to the philosophy of education.* New York: Macmillan Company.

Dickard, N. (Ed.). (2003). *The sustainability challenge: Taking edtech to the next level.* Washington, DC: Benton Foundation.

Domine, V. (2002). "We're wired! Now what?" A holistic approach to technology planning in high schools. *Journal of Literacy and Technology, 2*(2). Retrieved November 21, 2007 from http://www.literacyandtechnology. org/v2n2/domine/domine.htm.

Domine, V. (2004). How important is technology in urban education? In S. Steinberg & J. Kincheloe (Eds.). *19 Urban questions: Teaching in the city* (pp. 210–218). New York: Peter Lang.

Domine, V. (2006a). "Doing technology" in the college classroom: Media literacy as critical pedagogy. In R. Goldstein (Ed.). *Useful theory: Making critical education Practical* (pp. 131–147). New York: Peter Lang.

Domine, V. (2006b) Four steps to standards integration. *Learning and Leading with Technology, 34*(3), 22–25.

Domine, V. (2006c). Student attitudes towards internet use at school. *Academic Exchange Quarterly, 10*(2), 104–108.

Domine, V. (2007). Commerce in schools: Four U.S. perspectives. *Society and Business Review, 2*(1), 98–120.

Donaldson-Evans, C. (2004, September 23). Schools make rules for cell phone no-nos. Fox News. Retrieved April 25, 2005 from http://www.foxnews.com/story/0,2933,133208,00.html.

Edwards, V. B. (Ed.) (2006, May 4). Technology counts 2006: The information edge. *Education Week, 25*(35). Entire issue.

Ellul (1964). *The technological society*. New York: Knopf.

Ellul (1980). *The technological system*. New York: Continuum.

Erickson, C. G. (1964). The administrator, educational problems, and instructional television. In R. M. Diamond (Ed.), *A guide to instructional television* (pp. 172–179). New York: McGraw-Hill Book Company.

Fass, P. (1977). *The damned and the beautiful: American youth in the 1920s*. New York: Oxford University Press.

Fass, P. (1991). *Outside in: Minorities and the transformation of American education*. New York: Oxford University Press.

Federal Works Agency. (1940). *A list of free and inexpensive teaching materials*. Washington, DC: Works Project Administration, Division of Professional and Service Projects.

Feinberg, W. (2000). *Common schools/uncommon identities: National unity and cultural difference*. New Haven, CT: Yale University Press.

Finn, J. D. (1972). Automation and education: Technology and the instructional process. In R. J. McBeath (Ed.), *Extending education through technology: Selected writings by James D. Finn on instructional technology* (pp. 141–160). Washington, DC: Association for Educational Communications and Technology.

Fisherkeller, J. (1997, December). Everyday learning about identities among young adolescents in television culture. *Anthropology & Education, 28*(4), 467–492.

Fisherkeller, J. (2002). *Growing up with television: Everyday learning among young adolescents*. Philadelphia: Temple University Press.

Fiske, J. (1989). *Reading the popular*. Boston: Unwin Hyman.

Foucault, M. (1972). *The archeology of knowledge*. (A. M. Sheridan Smith, Trans.). New York: Pantheon Books.

Fox, R. (1995). *Harvesting minds: How TV commercials control kids*. New York: Praeger.

Friere, P. R. (2000). *Pedagogy of the oppressed* (3rd ed.). New York: Continuum.

Frith, K. T. (Ed.). (1997). *Undressing the ad: Reading culture in advertising.* New York: Peter Lang.

Fullan, M. (2007). *The new meaning of educational change* (4th ed.). New York: Teachers College Press.

Gadamer, H. G. (1975). *Truth and method.* (G. Barden & J. Cumming, Trans.). London: Sheed & Ward.

Geiger, K. (1995, October 25). Fed up with all the TV trash? Let's make the tube morally fit for our kids. *Education Week,* p. x.

George, R. G. (1991). Technology and teaching methodology. *Contemporary Education, 63*(1), 62–64.

Gilkey, R. (1970, November). Instructional media: Considerations for administrators when big business moves into education. *The Clearing House,* pp. 43–51.

Gong, E. J. (1996, April 1). Lessons laced with ads used in more classrooms: Corporate-sponsored teaching aids pitch products to students. *The Seattle Times,* p. 26.

Goodlad, J. I. (2006, March). *The Goodlad occasional, 1*(1), 1–3.

Goodman, N. (1978). *Ways of worldmaking.* Indianapolis, IN: Hackett Publishing Company.

Google enrolls teachers in online software crusade. (2006, December 17). *Cable News Network (CNN).* Retrieved December 17, 2006 from http://www.cnn.com.

Gore, A. (1998, March 23). Statement of the vice president on protecting our children from inappropriate material on the internet (Press Release).

Goulart, R. (1969). *The assault on childhood.* London: Lowe & Brydone.

Gozzi, Jr., R., & Haynes, W. L. (1992). Electric media and electric epistemology: Empathy at a distance. *Critical Studies in Mass Communication, 9*(3), 217–228.

Grahame, J. (1992). Doing advertising. *The English and Media Magazine,* pp. 34–39.

Gramsci, A. (1971). *Selections from prison notebooks.* New York: International Publications.

Greenwood, V. E. (1994). Communication, education and technology: A critical discourse analysis of the local Channel One controversy. Unpublished master's thesis, San Jose State University, Department of Communication Studies.

Habermas, J. (1971). *Knowledge and human interests.* (J. J. Shapiro, Trans.). Boston: Beacon Press.

Hall, S. (1973). Encoding and decoding in the television message. In S. Hall, D. Hobson, A. Lowe, & P. Willis (Eds.). (1980). *Culture, media, language.* London: Hutchinson.

Hall, S. (1974). Encoding and decoding. *Education and culture*. Birmingham, England: Centre for Cultural Studies.

Haney, J. M. (1989, November). TV 101: Good broadcast journalism for the classroom? Paper presented at the annual meeting of the Speech Communication Association, San Francisco, CA.

Harris, D. N., & Herrington, C. D. (2006, February). Accountability, standards, and the growing achievement gap: Lessons from the past half century. *American Journal of Education, 11*(2).

Harris, N. E. (1975). *A study of certain critical thinking skills among fifth-graders in the area of propaganda in advertising*. Unpublished doctoral dissertation. Boston University School of Education.

Hart Research Associates. (2007, October 10). *U.S. students need 21st century skills to compete in a global economy*. Retrieved November 20, 2007 from http://www. 21stcenturyskills.org/documents/P21_pollreport_singlepg.pdf

Harty, S. (1979). *Hucksters in the classroom: A review of the industry propaganda in schools*. Washington, DC: Center for Study of Responsible Law.

Hawkins, J. (1990). *Design experiments: Integrating interactive technology into classrooms*. Paper presented at the annual meeting of the American Educational Research Association, Boston, MA.

Hawkins, R. P., & Pingree, S. (1982). Television's influence on social reality. In D. Pearl, L. Bouthilet, & J. Lazar (Eds.). *Television and behavior: Ten years of scientific progress and implications for the eighties* (Vol. 2, pp. 224–247). Rockville, MD: National Institute of Mental Health.

Hayakawa, S. I. (1964). *Language in thought and action*. New York: Harcourt, Brace and World.

Hays, C. L. (1998a, March 10). Battle for soft-drink loyalties moves to public schools. *The New York Times*. Retrieved March 10, 1999 from http://www.nytimes.com.

Hays, C. L. (1998b, May 21). Today's lesson: Soda rights. *The New York Times*, B1,9.

Hecker, D. E. (2005, November). Occupational employment projections to 2014. *Monthly Labor Review Online, 128*(11). Retrieved October 20, 2007 from http://www.bls.gov/opub/mlr/2005/11/art5full.pdf.

Heins, M., & Cho, C. (2003). *Media literacy: An alternative to censorship* (2nd ed.). New York: Free Expression Policy Project.

Heintz, K. E. (1994). Smarter than we think—Kids, passivity and the media. *Media Studies Journal, 8*(4), 205–219.

Herrera, J. M. (1993, June 3). *Channel One—Whittle Communications*. Unpublished document.

Hobbs, R. (1998). The uses (and misuses) of mass media resources in secondary schools. Retrieved January 7, 1999 from http://interact. uoregon.edu/MediaLit/FA/mlhobbs/uses.html.

Honey, M., & Moeller, B. (1990). *Teachers' beliefs and technology integration: Different values, different understandings.* CTE Technical Report No. 6. Center for Technology in Education.

Honey, M., & Shookhoff, C. (Eds.). (2000). *A summary report of the Wingspread Conference on technology's role in urban school reform: Achieving equity and quality.* New York: EDC Center for Children and Technology.

Hoynes, W. (1997). News for a captive audience: An analysis of Channel One. *Extra: The magazine of FAIR, 10*(3), 11–17.

Hurst, M. D. (2005, May 5). Technology counts 2005: Electronic Transfer. *Education Week, 24*(35), 34–36, 39.

iPod sparks enthusiasm among ELL students. Retrieved January 4, 2007 from http://www.apple.com/education/profiles/grandisland/.

Jenkins, H., Clinton, K., Purushotma, R., Robinson, & A. J., Weigel, M. (2006). *Confronting the challenges of participatory culture: Media education for the 21st century.* Chicago: MacArthur Foundation.

Karpatkin, R. H., & Holmes, A. (1995, September). Making schools ad-free zones. *Educational Leadership, 53*(1), 72–76.

Kearney, C. A. (2000). *Curriculum partner: Redefining the role of the library media specialist.* Westport, CT: Greenwood Press.

Kemp, J. E. (1964). Television: Part of the answer. In R. M. Diamond (Ed.), *A guide to instructional television* (pp. 180–191). New York: McGraw-Hill Book Company.

Kirkpatrick, M. (2006, July 11). MySpace hit #1 US destination last week, Hitwise. *TechCrunch.* Retrieved November 1, 2007 from http://www.techcrunch.com/2006/07/11/myspace-hit-1-us-destination-last-week-hitwise.

Klem, A. M., & Connell, J. P. (2004, March). *Relationships matter: Linking teacher support to student engagement and achievement.* Paper presented at the Tenth Biennial Meeting of the Society for Research on Adolescence, March 11–14, Baltimore, MD.

Kliebard, H. M. (2004). *The struggle for the American curriculum: 1893–1958* (3rd ed.). New York: Routledge.

Kotter, J. P. (1999). *What leaders really do.* Cambridge, MA: Harvard University Press.

Kozol, J. (1992, September 21). Whittle and the privateers. *The Nation, 255*(8), 272–278.

Krich, P. (1969). Education: Servant of industry. *School & Society, 97*(2318), 280–281.

Kuntz, M., Weber, J., & Dawley, H. (1996, July 1). The new hucksterism. *Business Week,* pp. 76–84.

Lamb, B. (2004). Wide open spaces: Wikis, ready or not. *EDUCAUSE Review, 39*(5), 36–48.

Lathrop, A., & Foss, K. (2000). *Student cheating and plagiarism in the internet era: A wake-up call.* Westport, CT: Libraries Unlimited.

Lenhart, A. (2007, June 27). *Data memo: Cyberbullying and online teens.* PEW Internet & American Life Project. Retrieved October 30, 2007 from http://www.pewinternet.org/pdfs/PIP%20Cyberbullying%20Memo.pdf.

Lenhart, A., Rainie, L., & Lewis, O. (2001). *Teenage life online: The rise of the instant-message generation and the internet's impact on friendships and family relationships.* Washington, DC: Pew Internet and American Life Project.

Levin, D., Arafeh, S., Lenhart, A., & Rainie, L. (2002). *The digital disconnect: The widening gap between internet-savvy students and their schools.* Washington, DC: Pew Internet and American Life Project.

Levine, A. (2006). *Educating school teachers.* Washington, DC: Education Schools Project.

Lewis, J., Wahl-Jorgensen, K., & Inthorn, S. (2003). *Images of citizenship on television news: Breaking the cycle of decline in political participation.* Swindon, UK: Economic and Social Research Council (ESRC).

Liebert, R. M., Sprafkin, J. N., & Davidson, E. S. (1982). *The early window: Effects of television on children and youth* (2nd ed.). New York: Pergamon Press.

Livingstone, S., & Bovill, M. (Eds.). (2001). *Children and their changing media environment.* London: Lawrence Erlbaum Associates.

Livingstone, S., Bober, M., & Helpser, E. (2005, February). *Internet literacy among children and young people.* UK Children Go Online Project. Retrieved February 28, 2006 from http://personal.lse.ac.uk/bober/UKCGOfinalReport.pdf.

Marri, A. R. (2005). Educational technology as a tool for multicultural democratic education: The case of one US history teacher in an underresourced high school. *Contemporary Issues in Technology and Teacher Education, 4*(4), 395–409.

Maslow, A. (1987). *Motivation and personality* (3rd ed.). New York: Harper Collins College.

Masterman, L. (1988). *Teaching the media.* London: Routledge.

McAllister, M. P. (1996). *The commercialization of American culture: New advertising, control and democracy.* Thousand Oaks, CA: Sage.

McCloskey, P. J. (2006, October 1). The Blogvangelist. *Teacher Magazine.* Retrieved October 6, 2006 from http://www.teachermagazine.org/tm/articles/2006/10/0102richardson.h18.html.

McLuhan, M. (1964). *Understanding media: The extensions of man.* New York: Bantam.

McNeal, J. U. (1987). *Children as consumers: Insights and implications.* Lexington, MA: Lexington Books.

Means, B., Penuel, W. R., & Padilla, C. (2001). *The connected school: Technology and learning in high school.* San Francisco: Jossey-Bass.

Medsger, B. (1976, December). The "free" propaganda that floods the schools. *The Progressive, 40*(12), 42–46.

Meier, D. (2007). Habits of mind. Coalition of essential schools national web. Retrieved October 2, 2007 from http://www.essentialschools.org/pub/ces_docs/about/phil/habits.html.

Miniwatts Marketing Group (MMG). (2006). World internet usage and population statistics. Retrieved June 14, 2006 from http://www.internetworldstats.com/stats.htm.

Mishra, P., & Koehler, M. J. (2006). Technological pedagogical content knowledge: A framework for teacher knowledge. *Teachers College Record, 108*(6), 1017–1054.

Molnar, A. (1992). Fears about business involvement. *Rethinking schools, 7*(1), 7.

Molnar, A. (1995, September). Schooled for profit. *Educational Leadership, 53*(1), 70–71.

Molnar, A. (1996). *Giving kids the business: The commercialization of America's Schools.* Boulder, CO: Westview Press.

Montgomery, K. C. (2002, November 30). Children in the digital age. *The American Prospect.* Retrieved August 14, 2008 from http://www.prospect.org/cs/articles?article=children_in_the_digital_age.

Morgan, M. (1993). *Channel One in the public schools: Widening the gaps.* A research report prepared for UNPLUG. Amherst: University of Massachusetts, Department of Communication.

Mumford, L. (1963). *Technics and civilization.* New York: Harcourt Brace Jovanovich. (Original work published in 1934).

Nader, R. (1974, October). Corporate propaganda goes to schools. *American Teacher, 59*(2), 7.

Nardi, B. A., & O'Day, V. L. (1999). *Information ecologies: Using technology with heart.* Cambridge, MA: MIT Press.

National Center for Education Evaluation (NCEE). (2007, March). *Effectiveness of reading and mathematics software products: Findings from the first student cohort.* Washington, DC: United States Department of Education.

National Center for Education Statistics (NCES). (2002, September). *Internet access in U.S. public schools and classrooms: 1994–2001.* Washington, DC: U.S. Department of Education.

National Educational Technology Standards for Administrators (NETS-A). (2002). Eugene, OR: International Society for Technology in Education (ISTE).

National Educational Technology Standards for Students (NETS-S). (2007). Eugene, OR: International Society for Technology in Education (ISTE).

National Educational Technology Standards for Teachers (NETS-T). (2008). Eugene, OR: International Society for Technology in Education.

National School Boards Association (2007, December). Social homework? *Scholastic Parent & Child, 15*(4), 54.

National Science Foundation (NSF). (2006, February). Science and Engineering Indicators 2006. Arlington, VA: Division of Science Resources Statistics.

National Survey of Student Engagement (NSSE). (2006). *Engaged learning: Fostering success for all students. Annual Report 2006.* Bloomington, IN: Indiana University Center for Postsecondary Research.

New Jersey State Department of Education (2005). *Core Curriculum Content Standards: Technological Literacy.* Retrieved October 20, 2007 from http://www.state.nj.us/education/cccs/s8_tech.htm.

Nichols, R. G. (1990, November). A challenge to current beliefs about educational technology. *Educational Technology, 30*(11), 24–28.

Oblinger, D. (2003). Boomers, Gen-Xers, and millennials: Understanding the new students. *EDUCAUSE Review, 38*(4), 36–45.

O'Hair, M. J., McLaughlin, H. J., & Reitzug, U. C. (2000). *Foundations of democratic education.* New York: Harcourt.

Oliver, J. W. (1956). *History of American technology.* New York: Ronald Press Company.

Online "teenangels" protect peers (2001, July 19). Cable News Network (CNN). Retrieved July 20, 2001 from http://fyi.cnn.com/2001/fyi/teachers.ednews/ 07/19/online.angels.ap/index.html.

Packard, V. (1957). *The hidden persuaders.* New York: David McKay & Company.

Palloff, R. M., & Pratt, K. (1999). *Building learning communities in cyberspace: Effective strategies for the online classroom.* San Francisco: Jossey-Bass.

Parker, W. C. (2002). *Teaching democracy: Unity and diversity in public life.* New York: Teachers College Press.

Pasnik, S. (2007). *iPod in education: The potential for teaching and learning.* New York: Center for Children and Technology.

Perlstein, L. (2004, January 18). Talking the edutalk: Jargon becoming prevalent in the classroom. *Washington Post,* p. A01.

Philly teacher assaulted over iPod (2007, February 24). News Release. Associated Press.

Poling, C. (2005). Blog on: Building communication and collaboration among staff and students. *Learning and Leading with Technology, 32*(6), 12–15.

Postman, N. (1970). The reformed English curriculum. In A. C. Eurich (Ed.), *High school 1980: The shape of the future in American secondary education* (pp. 160–168). New York: Pitman Publishing.

Postman, N. (1985). *Amusing ourselves to death*. New York: Penguin Books.

Postman, N. (1995). *The end of education: Redefining the value of school*. New York: Alfred A. Knopf.

Prensky, M. (2001). Digital natives, digital immigrants. On the Horizon. *NCB University Press, 9*(5).

Raup, B. (1936). *Education and organized interests in America*. New York: G. P. Putnam's Sons.

Report to the legislature on commercialism in schools. (1991). Olympia: Washington Office of the State Superintendent of Public Instruction. ED 33 23 01.

Rheingold, H. (1993). *The virtual community: Homesteading on the electronic frontier*. New York: HarperCollins.

Richardson, W. (2006). *Blogs, wikis, podcasts, and other powerful web tools for classrooms*. Thousand Oaks, CA: Corwin Press.

Rockoff, J. E. (2004). The impact of individual teachers on student achievement: Evidence from panel data. *The American Economic Review, 94*(2), 247–252.

Ruckdeschel, C. (2006). *Comparison of digital literacy development between children and adolescents*. Retrieved June 8, 2007 from http://www.teach-nology.com/tutorials/teaching/compare/.

Rushkoff, D. (1996). *Playing the future: How kids' culture can teach us to thrive in an age of chaos*. New York: HarperCollins.

Russell, M., Bebell, D., O'Dwyer, L., & O'Connor, K. (2003). Examining teacher technology use: Implications for preservice and inservice teacher preparation. *Journal of Teacher Education, 54*(4), 297–310.

Sanchez, R. (1998, March 9). A corporate seat in public classrooms: Marketing efforts bring revenue, opposition. *Washington Post*. Retrieved March 10, 1998 from http://www.washingtonpost.com

Sanders, W. L., & Horn, S. P. (1998). Research findings from the Tennessee Value-Added Assessment System (TVAAS) database: Implications for educational evaluation and research. *Journal of Personnel Evaluation in Education, 12*(3), 247–256.

Sandholtz, J. H., Ringstaff, C., & Dwyer, D. C. (1997). *Teaching with technology: Creating student-centered classrooms*. New York: Teachers College Press.

Sawicky, M. B.; & Molnar, A. (1998, April). *The hidden costs of Channel One: Estimates for the fifty states*. Milwaukee, WI: Center for the Analysis of Commercialism in Education.

Schiller, H. I. (1989). The corporate capture of the sites of public expression. *Culture, Inc.: The corporate takeover of public expression*. (pp. 89–110). New York: Oxford University Press.

Schofield, J. W., (2003, November). Bringing the internet to schools effectively. *The Evolving Internet: Global Issues, 8*(3). Retrieved April 21, 2006 from http://usinfo.state.gov/journals/itgic/1103/ijge/gf09.html.

Schön, D. A. (1983). *The reflective practitioner: How professionals think in action.* New York: Basic Books.

Sclove, R. E. (1995). *Democracy and technology.* New York: Guilford Press.

Searle, J. R. (1995). *The construction of social reality.* New York: Free Press.

Shaw, D. E. (1998). Report to the president on the use of technology to strengthen K-12 education in the United States. *Journal of Science Education and Technology, 7*(2), 115–126.

Sinclair, T. J. (1949). *A report about business-sponsored teaching aids.* Dansville, NY: F. A. Owen Publishing Company.

Singhal, A.; Cody, M. J., & Rogers, E. M. (Eds.). (2003). *Entertainment-education and social change: History, research, and practice.* Mahwah, NJ: Lawrence Erlbaum Associates.

Skinner, B. F. (1958). Teaching machines. *Science, 128*, 969–977.

Smith, H. J. (1928). *Teaching aids for the asking.* Minneapolis, MN: University of Minnesota Press.

Social networking for the at-risk (2007, December). *American School Board Journal, 194*(12), 9.

Southern Region Educational Board (SREB). (2007). EvaluTech technology and literacy skills standards. Retrieved November 1, 2007 from http://www.evalutech.sreb.org/21stcentury/Standards.asp.

Sproule, J. M. (1994). *Propaganda.* Boston, MA: Cambridge University Press.

Sreberny-Mohammadi, A. (1995). Forms of media as ways of knowing. In J. Downing, A. Mohammadi, & A. Mohammadi (Eds.), *Questioning the media: A critical introduction* (2nd ed.) (pp. 23–37). London: Sage.

Stark, S. E. (1930). *The development of criteria for the educational evaluation of advertising material used by home economics workers.* New York: Association of National Advertisers.

Starkman, N. (2007). Ready for their closeups. *T.H.E. Journal, 34*(11), 24–25.

State Educational Technology Directors Association (SETDA). (2007). *2007 National Trends Report.* Retrieved February 28, 2008 from http://www.setda.org/web/guest/2007NationalTrendsReport

Strasburger, V. C. (1995). *Adolescents and the media: Medical and psychological impact.* Thousand Oaks, CA: Sage.

Strasburger, V. C., & Brown, R. T. (1991). *Adolescent medicine: A practical guide.* Boston: Little, Brown.

Sturgeon, J. (2008). Five don'ts of classroom blogging. *T.H.E. Journal, 35*(2), 26–30.

Suárez-Orozco, M. M., & Gardner, H. (2002, April). Education for globalization. Paper presented at Pocantico Conference, Tarrytown, NY.

Suárez-Orozco, M. M., & Hilliard-Qin (Eds.). (2004). *Globalization: Culture and education in the new millennium.* Berkeley: University of California Press.

Susman, W. I. (1984). *Culture as history: The transformation of American society in the twentieth century.* New York: Pantheon Books.

Tannen, D. (1989). *Talking voices: Repetition, dialogue and imagery in conversational discourse.* New York: Cambridge University Press.

Tapscott, D. (1998). *Growing up digital: The rise of the net generation.* New York: McGraw-Hill Book Company.

Turkle, S. (1995). *Life on the screen: Identity in the age of the internet.* New York: Simon & Schuster.

Tyack, D. (2003) *Seeking common ground: Public schools in a diverse society.* Cambridge, MA: Harvard University Press.

Tyack, D. (2007). *The one best system: A history of American urban education.* Cambridge, MA: Harvard University Press.

Tyner, K. (1998). *Literacy in a digital world: Teaching and learning in the age of information.* Mahwah, NJ: Lawrence Erlbaum Associates.

United States Department of Education (USDOE). (2002). *No Child Left Behind.* Retrieved April 3, 2003 from http://www.nochildleftbehind. gov.

United States Department of Education (USDOE). (2004). *National Educational Technology Plan.* Retrieved September 1, 2006 from http://www.ed.gov/about/offices/list/os/technology/plan/2004/site/edlite-actionsteps.html.

Vygotsky, L. (1978). *Mind in society.* Cambridge, MA: Harvard University Press.

Walsh, D. (1994). *Selling out America's children: How America puts profits before values—and what parents can do.* Minneapolis, NJ: Fairview Press.

Walsh, M. (1999, April 7). Conservatives join effort to pull the plug on *Channel One. Education Week.* Retrieved June 1, 1999 from http://www.edweek.com/ew/vol-18/30tv.h18.

Whorf, B. L. (1964). *Language, thought, and reality: Selected writings of Benjamin Lee Whorf.* Cambridge, MA: MIT Press.

Willard, N. (2007). *The Julie Amero tragedy.* Center for Safe and Responsible Use of the Internet. Retrieved March 25, 2008 from http://csriu.org/onlinedocs/AmeroTragedy.pdf

Willard, N. (2008). Raises many questions. *Learning and Leading with Technology, 35*(6), 6.

Willis, P. (1990). *Common culture: Symbolic work at play in the everyday cultures of the young.* Buckingham: Open University Press.

Winn, M. (1977). *The plug-in drug.* New York: Viking Press.

Winner, L. (1986). *The whale and the reactor: A search for limits in an age of high technology.* Chicago: University of Chicago Press.

Index

Peter Lang
PRIMERS
in Education

Peter Lang Primers are designed to provide a brief and concise introduction or supplement to specific topics in education. Although sophisticated in content, these primers are written in an accessible style, making them perfect for undergraduate and graduate classroom use. Each volume includes a glossary of key terms and a References and Resources section.

Other published and forthcoming volumes cover such topics as:

- Standards
- Popular Culture
- Critical Pedagogy
- Literacy
- Higher Education
- John Dewey
- Feminist Theory and Education

- Studying Urban Youth Culture
- Multiculturalism through Postformalism
- Creative Problem Solving
- Teaching the Holocaust
- Piaget and Education
- Deleuze and Education
- Foucault and Education

Look for more Peter Lang Primers to be published soon. To order other volumes, please contact our Customer Service Department:

    800-770-LANG (within the US)
    212-647-7706 (outside the US)
    212-647-7707 (fax)

To find out more about this and other Peter Lang book series, or to browse a full list of education titles, please visit our website:

    www.peterlang.com